Harrison Birtwistle in
Recent Years

The Contemporary Composers

Series Editor: Nicholas Snowman

Harrison Birtwistle in Recent Years

Michael Hall

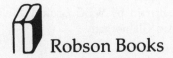

Robson Books

First published in Great Britain in 1998 by Robson
Books Ltd, Bolsover House, 5–6 Clipstone Street,
London W1P 8LE

British Library Cataloguing in Publication Data
A catalogue record for this title is available from the
British Library

ISBN 1 86105 179 4

Typeset in by Derek Doyle & Associates, Mold,
Flintshire, North Wales.
Printed by Great Britain by WBC Book Manufacturers
Ltd., Bridgend, Mid-Glamorgan

Contents

Editor's Preface

The Contemporary Composers series was first launched some fifteen years ago. In that time exceptional changes have taken place in the world of classical music. The traditional concert with its established repertoire based mainly in the eighteenth and nineteenth centuries is now showing signs of vulnerability, whereas contemporary music is flourishing in a way that would have been difficult to imagine in the early 1980s.

Until relatively recently music-lovers had.to come to concerts to hear unfamiliar repertoire. With the arrival of CDs, and in particular budget price reissues of superlative and celebrated recordings, acquainting oneself with, for example, a lesser known Dvorak symphony has become a far easier task than it was when there was no alternative but to catch a live performance. Now the public quite rightly wishes to experience major events rather than run of the mill evenings of classical or, indeed, any other music. The future must surely lie in the presentation of fewer but more stimulating concerts.

These past fifteen years have also seen the arrival in prominent positions of conductors with a greater sense of adventure and idealism than most of their predecessors. The two most potent symbols of status quo and tradition in classical music, the Berlin Philharmonic and the Vienna Philharmonic, have both undergone profound transformation. Not only are these orchestras now conducted by a range of musicians representing a new breadth of interpretative styles, but the players themselves have responded remarkably to change as well as bringing fresh young talent into their own ranks.

These changes are particularly marked in the United Kingdom where symphony orchestras have moved from simply replaying

the established canon of works to a broader repertoire including pieces from the post-Second World War and contemporary eras. Before, such repertoire had been left largely to the BBC. Now distinguished festivals devoted to contemporary work exist in Huddersfield and the Vale of Glamorgan, whilst arts centres and concert halls up and down the country demonstrate that the contemporary is ever more integrated with the traditional.

These developments are matched in the record industry. Though the attractiveness of reasonably priced reissues has rendered the endless re-recording of standard works uneconomical, this situation has encouraged companies to investigate the distant past as well as the present far more imaginatively than before. Of course, financial constraints are increasingly to be felt world-wide, but it is most encouraging to sense the new vigour in the promotion of contemporary work internationally.

When these books were first launched, not only was the situation for contemporary music less healthy than today but some of the composers we featured, for example, Birtwistle, Ligeti and Maxwell Davies, whilst known to a specialist international audience, were not the familiar names they have now become. Hopefully, this series will continue to play a modest but precise role in increasing the enjoyment of the music it celebrates.

Nicholas Snowman
London

Acknowledgements

I am particularly indebted to David Beard who read the text and made several extremely useful suggestions for improvement. My thanks also to Robert Adlington who got me started and whose thesis I raided; to Robert Piencikowski of the Paul Sacher Foundation who was so helpful to me in Basel; to Miranda Jackson and Elke Hockings of Universal Edition, and David Allenby and Emma Carr of Boosey and Hawkes, who provided me with scores and information; to Brenda, my wife, for her encouragement and editing skills, and, not least, to Harry himself.

This book would have been impossible to publish without the kind permission of Boosey and Hawkes to reprint the example from *Exody*, and to Universal Edition (London) for their equally kind permission to reprint Harry's texts for *Songs by Myself* and musical examples from *Antiphonies, Earth Dances, Endless Parade, Four Poems by Jaan Kaplinski, Four Songs of Autumn, Gawain, La Plage, Nacht, Nenia, Ritual Fragment, Salford Toccata, Secret Theatre, Songs by Myself, Tenebrae, The Second Mrs Kong* and *Yan Tan Tethera*.

Introduction

When Birtwistle talks about his music it is usually about those aspects currently absorbing him. He never provides you with a comprehensive overview. Imagine my surprise then when, in December 1997, during our conversation about his orchestral work *Exody* (103)* which he had just completed, he said he wanted to try and put into a few words what was common to all the works he had composed. At first he came up with 'a continuity that's been fractured', 'a logic that's been disturbed'. Then he remembered what the painter Francis Bacon had said about his aims: 'What I've always wanted to do is to make things that are very formal yet coming to pieces.'†

I had hoped he would amplify this statement by giving me various examples of how it applies to his music, but as always he restricted himself to one aspect of the work which had been preoccupying him for more than a year. 'If I sketch a passage either in my head or on paper that consists, say, of seven phrases or ideas in which one leads smoothly and logically into the next, I break these up when I come to compose the work and reorder the events. The logical sequence is still there, but it has been fractured, disturbed, messed up. Alternatively I might sketch two logical sequences, let's say ABCDE and VWXYZ, and then inter-

---

* Numbers in brackets refer to the order in which works appear in the Catalogue on pp.154, where more information can be found.
† Quoted in David Sylvester, *About Modern Art: Critical Essays 1948–96*, Chatto and Windus, London 1996, p.173.

lock them to produce AVBWCDXYEZ. These processes are how I compose most of my melodies, rhythmic patterns, and at a structural level, the long line that runs right through *Exody*.'

When I started writing my first book about Birtwistle in 1979 this information would have been invaluable. Unfortunately it was withheld as were other crucial aspects of his technique. I think at that time Birtwistle thought they were self-evident. Although I did manage to unravel these dislocating processes eventually, there always came a moment in my attempts to analyse his music when I was utterly floored by some incongruity. None of the standard methods employed to analyse music were of any use. It was clear I had failed to comprehend the full extent of what I now know to be his 'messing up' processes. I grasped the fact that his music is a combination of medieval techniques (*cantus firmus*, *organum*, isorhythm, hocketing) and twentieth-century interests such as symmetrical pitch formations and additive rhythms, but these were no help in explaining the degree of inexplicable caprice in his scores.

That he was deliberately holding something back became clear one evening at dinner when Sheila, his wife, asked him if he had shown me the sheaves of numbers he was always consulting, and he abruptly changed the subject. I later discovered when he dipped into one of his drawers and gave me a handful of sketches that these were random numbers. They constituted his prime method of messing things up. A logical sequence of pitches or durations, for example, would be arranged in an order that he had either selected from his list or hit upon willy-nilly. It was on the information I gained from these sketches (some of them little more than a page or two) that I was able to write my book.* The version of something 'formal yet coming to pieces' that I coined when writing the study was what I rather pompously called his 'central organizing principle'. This was: 'start with an absolutely regular and uniform pattern of the simplest, most

* Michael Hall, *Harrison Birtwistle*, Robson Books, London, 1984.

predictable kind then superimpose upon it a pattern which is its extreme opposite – something capricious and unpredictable'.

Perhaps Birtwistle deliberately withheld information about his use of random numbers because he thought it might expose him to the accusation that he was not in control of what he did. However, when he knew that I was about to publish the information in my book he was perfectly willing to talk about his use of chance operations. In our conversation which ended the book he explained that they often produce the best result: 'I've noticed that when a group of actors walk on to a stage before a rehearsal and stop, the shape they'll make will be marvellous. But as soon as a stage director says "Could you come over here", or "Oh, I can't see him, will you stand there", or "Could we have the leading man down front", it's ruined.'

His main point was that his use of random numbers or chance operations did not mean he had forfeited all control over his material, and to illustrate this he cited the ritornellos in *Cantata* (28) and *Verses for Ensembles* (25), in which the conductor and players are free to choose from options he has given them. He argued that the ritornellos always sound the same no matter what the choice because the result depends on the number of players involved. He had been able to distance himself from 'the musical object', given it through the players a degree of autonomy so that that it had a life of its own – found a new perspective on it. 'But I've never lost control,' he said. 'That's the important thing.'

Thirteen years later, during the course of our initial conversation preparatory to writing the present book, the situation was totally different. It was he who broached the subject of chance, recommending me to read what Francis Bacon had to say about the matter ('as so often he had the words for what I really want to say'). He referred me to the interviews David Sylvester had conducted with Bacon and published under the title *The Brutality of Fact*.*

---

* David Sylvester, *The Brutality of Fact*, Thames and Hudson, London 1987.

Some of the remarks appearing to summarize Birtwistle's position are: 'If anything works for me, I feel it is nothing I have made myself, but something chance has been able to give me', 'I want a very ordered image but I want it to come about by chance', 'I know what I want to do but don't know how to bring it about. And that's what I'm hoping accidents or chance or whatever you like to call it will bring about for me', 'What so-called chance gives you is quite different from what willed application of paint gives you. It has an inevitability very often which the willed putting-on of paint doesn't give you'. 'What I call an accident may give you some mark that seems to be more real, truer to the image than another one, but it's only your critical sense that can select it', 'Half my painting is disrupting what I can do with ease', 'I'm not really trying to *say* anything, I'm trying to *do* something', 'I'm working for myself; what else have I got to work for? How can you work for an audience? What can you imagine that an audience would want?'

As well as Birtwistle's willingness to talk about his music without holding anything back, the writing of this book has been greatly aided by the public availability of most of his sketches. The handful I was given when writing the first book gave me only glimpses of his technique. I could not be sure that what he was doing on the one page I had of *Cantata* was applicable to all his music or not. But now that most of his sketches for works written since 1967 can be consulted, I know the way he put the melodic line together on that page was unique to the period when it was written.

The first sketches that became available for public perusal were those for *Secret Theatre* (65) which he gave to the Friends of the Musicians Benevolent Fund for their auction to raise funds for the charity in November 1987. They were bought by the British Library. Two years later, in December 1989, the Paul Sacher Foundation in Basel, Switzerland concluded an agreement with Birtwistle to acquire all the manuscripts and sketches he had in his possession at the time and would be producing in the future. One of the results was when he delved into his cupboards he found the score of *Three Sonatas for Nine Instruments* (3) which for years everybody thought had been lost.

Unfortunely he had retained none of his early sketches. The first extant are eleven pages for *Monodrama* (20), the work he wrote for the concert that launched the Pierrot Players in 1967 but subsequently withdrew. This means there are none for *Tragoedia* (14) or *Punch and Judy* (18), the pieces that established his reputation and represent his early style at its most arresting. Nevertheless most of the sketches for the works he composed after *Monodrama* are contained in the Swiss library. Apart from very short works which did not need sketching, those that are missing are the sketches for *La Plage* (44), which are in my possession, *Pulse Field* (51), *Four Songs of Autumn* (74) and *An die Musik* (75). The absence of those for *Four Songs of Autumn* is a great loss because Birtwistle considers the work summarizes all the technical procedures that preoccupied him in the late eighties.

However, very few of the sketches are complete. Sometimes only a page or two may be missing, but there are none for the first third of *Earth Dances* (69), nor for two of the *Three Movements for String Quartet* (89), nor for substantial sections of *The Second Mrs Kong* (90). Birtwistle can also be a little tardy in sending his manuscripts and sketches to Basel. When I was there in spring 1997, those for *The Second Mrs Kong,* which he had completed three years earlier, were the last he had submitted.

When studying his sketches it has to be borne in mind that he considers many of them to be simply 'ways of organizing my mind' prior to the act of composition. Several are intellectual abstractions that are too uninteresting musically to be of any value in themselves. Those that deal with the way musical shapes can be related and coordinated, which he worked on in 1969 and 1970, for instance, are merely models. When he came to actually write music based on them they are treated quite freely, as the example from *Cantata* on pages 55 and 56 of my first book illustrates. More recently, the strings of four-note arpeggios, which appear in his sketches and are clearly meant to be the basis of melodies as well as chords, also prove to be abstract procedures constructed for his imagination to work on.

As well as supplying a great deal of information about how he works out the details of a score, the sketches also reveal how his procedures have changed over the years. The most significant have been his dropping of pre-compositional planning and his adoption of a different procedure to get the process of composition under way. Up until the mid-seventies the starting point was almost inevitably a wedge-shaped pattern which starts with a single note then alternates a scale of rising semitones and a scale of falling semitones until all twelve notes of the chromatic scale have been involved. Since the mid-seventies, the starting point has varied. As often as not it is a scale or a set of scales that are modal in character. A prime example can be found on the first pages of his sketches for *Endless Parade* (71) where a series of seven-note scales are laid out, each containing a major third, two whole tones and three semitones in differing arrangements. Later the strings of four-note arpeggios mentioned above begin to appear. They too are calculated in terms of their intervals.

In my first book I was able to say that all Birtwistle's music, no matter how dense it may be, is a single line filled out by other lines moving in parallel motion with it or by heterophony – the presentation of differing versions of the same line simultaneously. To a large extent this continues to be true, but not always. In recent years pieces have emerged where the emphasis has been on rhythm rather than line. Ostinatos have become much more noticeable and much more dramatically important. And throughout the last fifteen years much more attention has been paid to harmony, in particular to the use of long-range harmony based on modal principles. As well as this several of his works have had their genesis in a chord that took his fancy as he improvised at the piano.

What the sketches are not concerned with, however, are what

one might call the higher things – the worlds that Birtwistle tries to create, his interest in the use of multiple perspectives or his preoccupation with time. In the early seventies, shortly before he wrote *The Triumph of Time* (43), he said, 'Music is the one medium where Time can transcend itself more than anything else. With poetry you are always up against language and meaning – in theatre too – while with painting you're up against the frame, which limits the size and scale. Time scale in music is something which has nothing to do with the length of a piece – and new concepts of Time are my main compositional preoccupation.'* The extent of his preoccupation reaches out to such things as pitting 'real' time against an abbreviated time scale, slow motion, accelerated motion, the way we experience time in dreams or in contemplation, the time shifts that occur when we rerun past events in our memories or anticipate what might happen in the future. The list is long, but perhaps the most persistent has been his preoccupation with the avoidance of 'goal orientation'.

By 'goal orientation' Birtwistle means the way tonal music in particular establishes a clear temporal aim (a firm tonic cadence) and strives to achieve it. This is something that composers such as Webern, Messiaen and John Cage also wanted to get away from. But Birtwistle is essentially a dramatic composer, and by its very nature drama must move in a purposeful direction. His solution has been to compose music in which the purposeful direction is inhibited. This is one of the reasons why he breaks up a logical sequence of events and reorders them. On a broader perspective he achieves similar results by superimposing on the necessary linear progression a repetitive, cyclic process. In his early music the cyclic process was given priority, but later its pre-eminence gave way to a more directional continuity. Nowhere is this shift of emphasis clearer than in his operas. The first two, *Punch and Judy* (18) and *The Mask of Orpheus* (60), are dominated

---

* Quoted by Michael Nyman in his sleeve note for *The Fields of Sorrow* (39), recorded by Decca on Head 7.

by cyclic processes. But in *Gawain* (81) they are confined mainly
to two scenes, while in *The Second Mrs Kong* (90) they appear only
at the beginning and are the object of comedy.

Yet this should not deceive us into thinking that Birtwistle has
fallen in line with traditional linear procedures – far from it.
During our conversation about *Exody* in December 1997, he
presented me with another quotation which put into words what
he wanted to say about his music. This one comes from the
psychologist, Bruno Bettelheim, who was internationally known
for his work with autistic children: 'All autistic children demand
that time must stop still,' he wrote. 'Time is the destroyer of
sameness. If sameness is to be preserved, time must stop still in
its tracks... In the autistic child's world the chain of events is
not conditioned by causality we know. But since one event does
follow another, it must be because of some timeless cosmic law
that ordains it. An eternal law. Things happen because they
must, not because they are caused.'*

* Quoted by Richard Davenport-Hines in his biography of W.H. Auden,
Heinemann, London 1995, p.21.

1
1983–1986

In 1983 Birtwistle gave up his job as music director of the National Theatre and moved to rural France where he was able to devote himself exclusively to composition. During the following three years he produced six works and in each of them he broke new ground. Never before had he made so many changes to his compositional procedures, not even during the period between January 1969, when he completed *Verses for Ensembles* (25), and November 1970, when *Nenia: The Death of Orpheus* (34) had its first performance. These are the works which marked the transition from the iconoclastic music he composed in the sixties to the much more mellow music he produced in the seventies, when the Orpheus legend dominated his thoughts. In that earlier period, the change was one of mood, whereas in the period between 1983 and 1986, it was much more to do with relationships within his music. Crucial to these was what he called 'the sanctity of the context'. This led in turn to a change in his working methods, a reassessment of the relationship between the cyclic and linear processes in his music, a much clearer distinction between melody and accompaniment, a renewed interest in song writing, and the discovery that he could adopt a more traditional approach to long-range harmony without having to return to the so-called 'functional' aspects of modal or tonal harmonic practices. All these developments reflect the unwavering self-confidence he acquired during these years. With them he gained the maturity of style that has placed him at the peak of his profession.

THE SANCTITY OF THE CONTEXT

In December 1983, when I went to Lunegarde in Lot to record our conversations for the final section of my first book about him, he was about three-quarters of the way through his television opera *Yan Tan Tethera* (63). It had been commissioned by Radio 3 and BBC 2 some four years earlier for a simultaneous broadcast on both networks sometime in the autumn of 1984. He had been in possession of Tony Harrison's libretto★ since April 1980, but had to postpone writing the music until the much more pressing task of finishing *The Mask of Orpheus* (60) had been accomplished. Tony Harrison and he had been friends and colleagues for several years. Harrison had supplied the texts for *Bow Down* (52) and ... *agm* ... (54), and Birtwistle had composed the music for the production of Harrison's translation of *The Oresteia* at the National Theatre. The poet knew therefore that, among other things, Birtwistle required texts containing a great deal of varied repetition. *Bow Down* is based on different versions of the traditional ballad of 'The Two Sisters' so that during the course of the work we see and hear the same things from a variety of perspectives. But for *Yan Tan Tethera* it was decided that the repetitions should be an essential ingredient of the story itself.

The initial idea for the work was probably suggested by *The Magic Roundabout*, the popular children's television programme. The plot concerns a shepherd from the north who settles in Wiltshire and whose success in rearing sheep arouses the jealousy of a local shepherd. The set has to be built on a revolve containing two hills representing the ancient burial mounds of Wiltshire, each of which should also revolve. In doing so they indicate the turning of the seasons. The background to the story comes from folk tales about people ensnared in the mounds by fairies or the devil. But the most powerful magic is produced by

★ First published by Bloodaxe Books,1985. Now available in *Tony Harrison: Theatre Works 1973–1985*, published by Penguin Books, 1986.

the way Alan, the northern shepherd, counts. He uses a traditional sheep-counting system of which Yan, Tan, Tethera are the first three numbers. Whenever Alan counts his sheep using this system his sheep multiply. Caleb Raven, the jealous local shepherd who occupies the hill opposite to Alan's, believes the counting is a charm, and calls on the devil to lure his rival into a mound and imprison him there. In the second part of the opera, Alan's place on the hill is taken by his wife Hannah. Her twin babies have also been spirited away by the devil, and during her lament for them, she counts out the number of years she has to wait for their return, her words being echoed by the Cheviot sheep using the northern system of counting. On each count the hills revolve until seven is reached. Traditionally seven and three are considered to be lucky numbers, and it is through their subsequent repetition that Alan and the twins are eventually set free. Afterwards Caleb Raven's greed results in his own imprisonment in the mound, and the opera ends with his voice repeating over and over again unlucky thirteen, the devil's number.*

In his stage directions Tony Harrison says that whenever a hill turns the figures on it must behave as if they were wound by clockwork and 'freeze'. The 'music of the hill' which accompanies these moments, he says, should evoke the mysterious nature of the mounds and be sung off-stage by the chorus who, with the aid of masks, have also to double as Wiltshire sheep and Cheviot sheep. When Birtwistle came to write his music, he decided to eliminate 'the music of the hill', partly because getting the chorus on and off stage in time would pose problems, but basically because the repetition of the same music would be an affront to the 'sanctity of the context'. He told me he did not want to pick up something he had dropped some time ago and slot it into a new context willy-nilly. For him the context had become unique. 'In the past,' he said, 'if seven "music of the

---

* The story reflects Birtwistle's preoccupation with numbers and that he too was born in the Pennines and later went to Wiltshire, where he lived from 1960 to 1966, and where he has now returned.

hills" were needed and each had to last about a minute, I'd have composed a stretch of music lasting seven minutes, cut it into seven sections and provided each section with a beginning and an end. This is how I composed *Verses for Ensembles*, probably the most extreme example of this way of proceeding.' He then added: 'but the new departures I've made in *Yan Tan Tethera* haven't arisen out of the blue, the seeds were planted some time back. They appear in the substructure of *The Mask of Orpheus*, and they're also in the Clarinet Quintet.'

In place of 'the music of the hill', Birtwistle composed instrumental 'pastorals' which come directly out of the music that precedes them and are quite different from each other. 'The sacred thing,' he said, 'is the context. As soon as I move, as soon as I make a gesture and move to another there's a situation with ramifications. Things I would never have thought of in the first place appear. To these I have a duty. They are highly potent. From then the formalism starts showing itself. There's certainly no pre-composition.'

NEW WORKING METHODS

That last remark refers to his earlier practice of generating all the material he needed for a work in advance of getting down to write the score. His sketches reveal that before 1977 these preparations were undertaken with great care and effort. The pre-compositional sketches for *An Imaginary Landscape* (38), his seventeen-minute work for brass, double basses and percussion dating from 1971, take up 190 pages, more than twice the amount he ultimately required for the final score or either of the drafts. A little less than half the sketches for it are concerned with rhythmical ideas and the proportions of the work, the rest are devoted to pitch. The first fifteen pages of these are contained in a sketch-book dated April 1970, along with his initial sketches for *Prologue* (37), the first, abandoned version of *The Triumph of Time* (43) and charts formalizing the various shapes or contours that can be obtained from the same set of notes. These charts provide an admirable illustration of the way he seeks to extract the maximum from the minimum.

He considers the basic rhythmic gesture to be the heartbeat and the basic melodic one a simple opening out from a single note to the semitone above it and then the semitone below it, or vice versa. But because his music makes use of all twelve notes of the chromatic scale, he extends this simple melodic opening out to make a symmetrical wedge-shaped pattern.

This pattern is the source of Birtwistle's pitch material for all the works he composed before *Melencolia 1* (48). In that, and in most of his subsequent works, other symmetrical formations have been preferred. Since 1976 he has drawn on this wedge-shaped formation only intermittently.

Its elaboration depends entirely on what he has in mind for the work or some particular passage within it. In his April 1970 sketchbook, he heads one idea for its elaboration 'chorale ground harmony', a chorale being for him a simple hymn-like passage harmonized by doubling the melody at the fourth, fifth, octave or notes adjacent to these, a practice he derived from medieval *organum*. There is no indication whether he intended it to be for *The Triumph of Time* or the chorale that ends *An Imaginary Landscape*, but in all probability it is an early idea for the latter. The process of elaboration involves rotating the wedge-shaped pattern, expanding it by repeating the notes within it systematically, and then changing their order. In this instance, the expansion involves repeating the last three notes in each five-note group before adding the next two. The sixth group takes the sequence back to its starting point so that the sequence forms a cycle which can be repeated. The next step is to change the order of the notes in accordance with the numbers he places above them. In each case the numbers are 2 4 5 3 1. This means, for example, that the order of the notes in the first five-note group will be A-B-C♯-C-B♭.

This set of numbers comes from tables of random numbers Birtwistle has been using since he started work on *Chorales* (7) in 1960. They were given to him by an old schoolfriend working at Imperial College. Random numbers have always played an important role in his technique, and before then he generated his own. On the evidence of his sketches, the tables he was given seem to consist only of sets of three, four, five, six and seven numbers. He usually uses them in conjunction with highly ordered and predictable patterns. The combination of these opposites constitute what I called in my first book his central organizing principle. The highly ordered patterns give his music an inner consistency, the random numbers a degree of spontaneity he feels he could never achieve himself. At one time I believed his central organizing principle governed all aspects of his music, but in recent years I have come to realize that it is just one aspect of a much broader principle, namely the juxtaposition of opposites.

When he selects a set of random numbers it may be by chance or by intention. It all depends on whether he wants to exercise a degree of control over the shape or contour of the phrase the numbers produce. As far as the 'chorale ground harmony' is concerned, I think he did. But when the sketches begin to deal specifically with *An Imaginary Landscape*, the sets of numbers were probably chosen quite arbitrarily. On one sheet he writes out twelve transpositions of the wedge-shaped pattern for each of the twelve brass instruments he is writing for: four trumpets, four horns, three trombones and a tuba. Each instrument also has its own mode of expansion and its own sets of random numbers. The first horn, for instance, starts on F♯ and proceeds in the following manner.

Birtwistle fails to indicate how this will be rhythmized, but he applies the same principle to durations as he does to pitch. The rhythmical equivalent of the highly predictable wedge-shaped pattern is a regular pulse. He has several ways in which it can be 'disturbed' or rendered more pliable or unpredictable. One is simply to superimpose on it another regular pulse moving at a different velocity, i.e. at a different tempo. This is the basis of most of *Chronometer* (41), *Silbury Air* (50) and *Pulse Sampler* (59). But the one he uses most frequently combines a regular pulse with an additive rhythm, a rhythm based on adding or subtracting units rather than multiplying or dividing them as used to be customary in Western music before the twentieth century. The most succinct example of his use of additive rhythms and the superimposition of different tempos occurs in a passage in *Nenia: The Death of Orpheus* (34), his dramatic scena for soprano, three clarinets, piano and crotales. It is the passage just before the

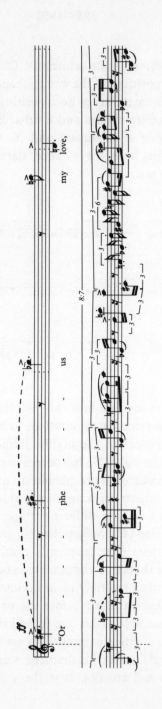

climax, when Orpheus is being torn apart by the Maenads and Euridice calls to him from across time and space. The basic pulse, a slow crotchet beat grouped into seven bars of 2/4, lies with the soprano. It is 'disturbed' partly by the addition of a quaver to the length of the fourth bar in order to delay and thus give emphasis to the words 'my love', but mainly by the very complex cross rhythm given to the clarinet representing the frenzy of the Maenads. Against the soprano's seven bars of 2/4 it has to fit eight groups of triplets, which means that the two are moving in the ratio of 7:8. Opposite are bars two, three, four and five of the passage. I have omitted the chord played by the piano and two bass clarinets on the fourth quaver of the 5/8 bar.

The sketch for the clarinet's line reveals that Birtwistle constructed it by superimposing three separate strands of ostinato on each other, and that he worked them out on a metric grid in which the clarinet's rhythm was aligned with the soprano's. The use of a metric grid was his standard practice. Here it relates everything in the passage to a regular pulse and makes it relatively easy to coordinate the ostinatos. In this instance the middle strand is an additive rhythm with a recurring semiquaver count of 1–3–2–3–1–2.

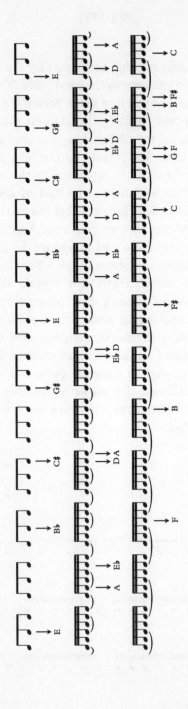

Superimposed on each of these strands is a melodic ostinato. The upper one rotates the notes C♯–G♯–E–B♭ across two octaves, the middle one E♭–D–A, the lower one G–F–E–F♯–C. But because Birtwistle wants the most frenzied activity to take place when the soprano sings 'my love' he accelerates the rotations towards this point, the middle strand consistently, the other two in stages. Opposite is how the four bars appear in the sketch.

It will be noticed that in several instances the final version differs from the sketch. This might be because as a clarinet player himself Birtwistle was aware of the technical difficulties the sketch version posed and wanted to make the final version more playable. Yet the more likely explanation is that as soon as he began to write out the final version he saw the musical improvements a few alterations would make, particularly to the shape of the phrase leading up to and away from 'my love'. Instead of jumping from register to register, the line now impetuously surges up to the apex of a single curve before falling away.

Nenia was composed for Jane Manning and a group called Matrix. Two years later, in 1972, when he wrote *La Plage* (44) for them, he produced the simplest example of his working methods. Usually the creation of a piece was undertaken in four stages. The first involved deciding on the nature of the work he wanted to write, its character and overall structure; the second entailed the generation of the material he would need; the third would be one or possibly two drafts of the work, each passage being preceded by additional, more detailed sketches; the fourth would be the meticulous final score. The first stage was usually worked out in his head. To the best of my knowledge, his initial ideas were committed to paper only once and that was when he came to write *Secret Theatre* (65). For *La Plage,* he had no need for a draft. His sketches are devoted entirely to the generation of the material, i.e. his 'pre-compositional' processes.

The title comes from a short story by Alain Robbe-Grillet about three children walking hand-in-hand along a deserted beach at noon on a summer's day. The regularity of their footsteps, the equally regular progress of a flock of birds along the beach and the lapping of the waves on the shore relate the situation to the orderly and predictable nature of Birtwistle's wedge-shaped pattern. The event that causes uncertainty is the sound of a distant bell. The seven brief remarks the children make in response to it convey the impression that they have been expecting it, but cannot remember whether they heard it earlier or not.

To turn the story into music Birtwistle had to find something else to replace the repetitive events on the beach since they would be virtually impossible to convey in sound. The idea that it should be an instrumental aria was a dramatic ploy, for normally in a work scored for voice and instruments the singer performs the aria. He subtitles the work 'eight arias of remembrance', partly because the children are trying to remember, but also, I suspect, because he could not get out of his mind the opera about Orpheus he was writing, and wanted to evoke the efforts of Orpheus to hold on to Euridice after he lost her the second time through 'arias of remembrance'. All those in *La Plage* are cast in floating additive rhythms; even the tolling of the bell is somewhat wayward. Between each of them the singer intones the seven remarks made by the children. However, little by little she gets drawn into what the instrumentalists are playing, and in the penultimate aria wanders through their notes singing wordlessly as if she were totally at one with them.

Of the seven pages of sketches devoted to generating the material, four are concerned with pitch, two with durations, the last with their combination. As with all Birtwistle's early music, the piece is essentially a monody, which means that all the harmonies and textures stem from a single melodic line. This applies even to the 'lovely chords' he mentions on the top left-hand corner of the first page, but fails to provide until the last. They are ultimately used in two of the arias for the sound of the bell.

I summarized the way the material was generated in my first book, but I want to go through it briefly again because I want to clear up a point about Birtwistle's use of numbers in the work, and I also want to explore more fully the implications of his procedures in general.

The 'lovely chords'.

I related the technique he employed on this paricular occasion to isorhythm, the highly economical medieval practice of combining a rotating melodic pattern of a certain length (*color*) with a rotating rhythmic pattern of a different length (*talea*) to produce a long line in which the repetitions are barely discernible. In this instance the *color* is the twelve-note wedge-shaped pattern, the *talea* a pattern of eight durations that get progressively longer.

TALEA

All Birtwistle needed for each of the arias was eight pitches and eight durations. For the first he used the first eight pitches in the wedge-shaped pattern, for the second, notes two to nine, for the third, three to ten, and so on. To expand this paucity of material he was inspired by the name of the group he was writing for in that he placed the eight pitches and eight durations in a matrix. This was designed to have them repeated eight times, each repetition being progressively shorter than the one before, until in the end only one pitch and one duration are left. The following is a combination of the pitch and duration matrices for the first aria. To obtain the notes it is necessary to read down each column in turn taking cognizance of the horizontal division and placing the notes in the order indicated by the numbers.

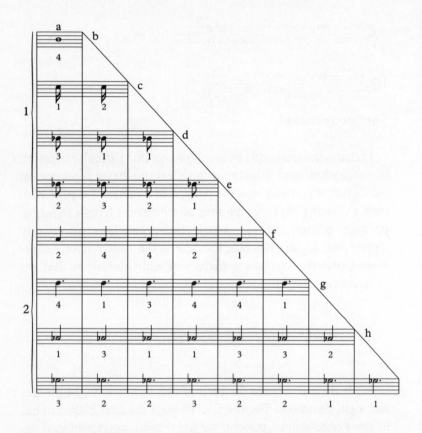

When he came to write out the line this produced he transposed everything down an octave, and in order to avoid having two Ds next to each other he reversed the D and E♭ in unit f2.

In the final score this is divided into two parts, the second beginning with unit d2 and containing the sound of the bell. The fact that d2 is a repetition of a2, makes it an excellent starting point for a new phrase. This raises the point about whether these numbers are random or not. One critic who reviewed my first book, a distinguished academic, thought they were logical and that Birtwistle must have selected them deliberately. He may well have done so, but nevertheless the logic is flawed. The permutation is far from consistent; there is a hint of caprice in its ordering.

Equally ambiguous is his approach to harmony. His use of symmetries such as the wedge-shaped pattern suggest that the harmonic pole of attraction in his music lies in the centre, in this case B. It has become a commonplace in twentieth-century harmonic practice to consider that a chord which is symmetric around a central axis sounds stable whatever its intervals. But although most of Birtwistle's music makes use of potentially symmetric formations, to the best of my knowledge the only time he has ever included a perfectly symmetric chord in his music is at letter E in *Refrains and Choruses* (1). It is a chord which has been carefully prepared and has D as its axis of symmetry. Its immediate effect is to trigger a disruptive solo for the horn, a solo which dramatically thrusts the music back to a state of instability. At the end of the piece, D reappears as the major third above B♭. Being symmetrically distributed around C, the note with which the work began, it could be argued that B♭ and D function as a 'frame' around the note which initiated the piece and that to round the work off Birtwistle has merely returned the work to its source. But C is not present at the end and it is doubtful whether anyone would hear the two notes other than as a bass-orientated concord that might end a modal or tonal work.

This is the clue to Birtwistle's harmonic thinking. Like just about everything he does it is based on the juxtaposition of opposites. In conversation he insists over and over again that essentially he is a modal composer who uses symmetric formations only to create the tension and the ambiguity he requires in his music. Modal and symmetric procedures are opposites in the sense that one builds its harmony from the bass upwards, the other from the centre outwards. However, the relationship between these contradictory procedures varies from piece to piece. In his early music, symmetric formations take precedence, the modal element appears only at or near the end of a work. Since then, as we shall see in the course of this book, the modal aspect of his thinking has become more evident. In addition to this, the relationship also depends on the degree of tension and ambiguity he needs for a particular work. When the tension has to be high, as in *Refrains and Choruses*, he veers towards symmetric formations. But on those occasions when the music can be more relaxed, such as in *La Plage*, the symmetrical formations are less in evidence and the modal sphere comes more to the fore. In some cases, especially when he is writing pieces for children such as *Sad Song* or *Berceuse de Jeanne* (67), the music is entirely modal.

The notes of the first aria in *La Plage* actually suggest a tonal context, particularly in the second part where the pianist's left hand supplies the tolling bell. The A♭ sounds like a tonic, the E♭ a dominant.

It must be borne in mind that all Birtwistle's music of the fifties, sixties and seventies is basically monody. The harmony comes out of the melody and is never independent. Apart from the punctuating chords in pieces such as *Verses for Ensembles* and *Imaginary Landscape* which often have a logic of their own, the

harmony comes out of the melody and is rarely independent of it. Sometimes it emerges from notes in the melody being sustained in another part, at other times from simultaneous variations of the melody (heterophony). But more often than not it is the result of the melody being doubled at the fourth, fifth or octave. When the harmony needs to be more astringent, he expands or narrows these intervals by a tone, semitone or even on occasions by a minor third. The choice of which adjacency he should use is often left to chance. In my first book I illustrated this with a passage from ... *agm.* .. (54) where he used random numbers. He has no need of these in *La Plage* because when the bell tolls in the first aria, for example, the basic chord is E♭–A♭–E♭ and the adjacencies to these notes are part of the melody.

In the story, there are two separate events – those that take place on the beach and the sounding of the bell. In the music, the two events are the arias and the sounding of the bell. The arias come out of the matrices, but the bell does not. Nevertheless it occurs whenever a certain note sounds in the aria. In the last, for instance, one of the 'lovely chords' is triggered every time an F sounds; in the second part of the first aria, the E♭–E dyad sounds whenever A♭ appears. This is why its pulse is so unsteady! But these are not the only events to be set off automatically. In the seventh aria the playing of a short note by the piano triggers the clarinets to double it at the fifth and then to sustain it. In this same aria just before an F♯ sounds in the piano, the marimba plays a fast, repeating pattern in its own tempo in imitation of the flock of birds flying to the next spot along the beach whenever the children come near them. The triggering devices may produce an automatic response, yet the results are wayward rather than mechanical. We are never quite sure when the bell will toll next or when the birds will take flight.

In his conversations with me at Lunegarde, Birtwistle gave me the impression that the 'pre-compositional' generation of material came to an end when he came to write *Yan Tan Tethera*. Yet the abandonment of this type of planning was not a sudden event. It took place over several years. His sketches reveal that the transition began in the mid-seventies. I was able to confirm that 'the sanctity of the context' is still his prime concern in autumn 1996 when I visited him in his new home in Wiltshire to discuss his future plans in readiness for writing this present book. He was then about two or three minutes into the orchestral piece he was composing for Daniel Barenboim and the Chicago Symphony Orchestra. A few weeks earlier he had been to Chicago to hear them rehearsing and performing *The Triumph of Time*, and this had given him the opportunity to get to know the musicians he was writing for. His provisional title for the new work was *Maze* and he wanted it to be a direct successor to *Earth Dances* (69), the big orchestral work he composed in 1985/6. His purpose, he said, was to write not only a virtuoso piece for a virtuoso orchestra, but to produce a work with a structure that kept on returning to material that sounds familiar, yet would nevertheless seem enigmatic.

The only pre-compositional sketch he had made for the work was a sheet devoted to a symmetrical 'abstract', in this case a chromatic scale ranging from the lowest note in the piece to the highest, a scale ranging from bottom C in double basses to the D six octaves above it. The axis of symmetry was the G above middle C, and he had divided the scale into groups of three or four notes coloured alternately orange and green. This was to enable him to see at a glance how a group in the lower register, for example, could be balanced by one in the upper one. The work opens with the note C being played at both extremes of this scale. After three bars the upper C moves up to the D. To fill in the gap he first of all introduces the central G played as a rhythmized pedal on the violins. Our conversation had turned to his use of random numbers, and to illustrate the fact that he now uses them only for aspects of detail and in a fairly controlled manner, he showed me his sketches for the passage where the violins begin to fan out from this central G. His scoring for the work has parts for only fifteen violins rather than the thirty or more normally found in a large symphony orchestra. On this occasion he wanted the first eight to play a series of undulating five-note scales, and the remaining seven to play a series of scales going down to the G an octave below. He also wanted the scales to be based on the harmonic minor scale, in that each should contain an augmented second (or minor third). He therefore selected seven sets of random numbers from 1 to 7, designating that 1, 3 and 5 would apply to where the semitones should be placed in each scale; 2, 4 and 6 to where the whole tones should be placed and 7 to the minor third. He then arranged the seven sets in an order in which 7 forms a diagonal running from the top left-hand corner to the bottom right-hand corner.

Line 1	7 5 1 4 2 6 3
Line 2	1 7 5 2 4 3 6
Line 3	4 2 7 1 3 5 6
Line 4	2 5 3 7 1 4 6
Line 5	2 4 6 3 7 1 5
Line 6	6 3 2 5 1 7 4
Line 7	3 1 4 6 5 2 7

This produces seven pairs of rushing scales, all beginning and ending on a G, and all different. In his first sketch for the passage he devised a numerical ordering for the two sets of scales, but he changed this when he came to write out the notes so that the first eight violins now play in succession lines 2 4 5 6 3 1 7 and the remaining violins lines 6 3 2 7 1 5 4. The passage involves only three and a half bars; accompanying the violins are rhythmically independent ostinatos on four trumpets and four percussion instruments, and a dense low chord on divided cellos and double basses.

Once the details have been worked, the gesture is written straight into the full score. Birtwistle rarely if ever has second thoughts. Although it is sometimes hard to believe, he claims that he never looks back to see what he did yesterday or the day before. For this reason he was at pains to emphasize that the sketches he showed me had to be taken only as an example of how he worked. He felt sure he had never done anything like it previously, nor does he intend to do so again. The context in which he found himself at that moment was unique.

THE BALANCE BETWEEN CYCLIC AND LINEAR PROCESSES

Although this is the first time he has used the word 'maze' as a metaphor for the form of a piece, the image of a labyrinth has always been of fundamental importance to him. It represents yet another instance of the juxtaposition of opposites, in this case the juxtaposition of cyclic and linear processes. He called *Silbury Air* (50), for example, a 'pulse labyrinth'. Its music undertakes three journeys through a network of metres only to find itself back where it started. In that sense it is cyclic. It is linear because the purpose of entering a labyrinth is to find a way out, and in the end the music achieves this goal. In most of his works composed before the mid-eighties, it is the cyclic rather than the linear, goal-orientated process which appear to be the most important aspect of the work's form. His commitment to cyclic forms arose in his student days when he first heard Satie's *Trois Gymnopédies*. Like most composers of his generation in the fifties, he had been searching for a form which expressed a sense of 'being' rather than 'becoming', and Satie's pieces achieve this state simply because they appear to be repetitions of the same thing heard from different perspectives. *La Plage*'s eight arias also encapsulate the idea of the same but always different. But unlike Satie, Birtwistle is a dramatic composer, and as such he cannot avoid incorporating into his music a sense of 'becoming'. In *La Plage* this linear process is given to the soprano. Yet in the eighth aria, after she has at last become at one with the instrumentalists, she returns to silence. In the end, it is the cyclic process that prevails.

The Triumph of Time, composed immediately before *La Plage*, terminates in a similar manner. Its proportions, however, are quite different because the cyclic event, a tune for the cor anglais which appears in varied forms near the beginning, in the middle and at the end of the work, takes up only two minutes of the work's half-hour duration. The bulk of the work consists of a string of musical events which, according to Birtwistle, 'have no necessary connections with each other'. Among them are a funeral march, sections of *Meridian* (36) and *The Fields of Sorrow* (39), a string chorale and *Chorale from a Toyshop* (19), a piece for wind instruments written for Igor Stravinsky's eighty-fifth birthday. But a string of unrelated events such as these cannot create a sense of purpose. To achieve this he introduces a three-note figure played seven times over the course of the work by an amplified soprano saxophone representing the angel of death in the Brueghel engraving on which the work is based. The tension comes from the fact that although the figure never changes, the listener knows it must. And when it does, it is transformed into a raucous chorale screamed out *fortissimo* by all the upper wood-wind. But it is not the ravages of time that bring the work to a close, it is the cor anglais sounding as if nothing had happened, as if nothing could disturb the inevitability of the 'eternal return'.

These cyclic processes come to a head in *Carmen Arcadiae Mechanicae Perpetuum* (53), a *bonne bouche* composed for the tenth anniversary of the London Sinfonietta in 1978. The idea for it came from Paul Klee's *The Twittering Machine*, but instead of four mechanical birds, Birtwistle's piece has six – 'six mechanisms juxtaposed many times without any form of transition'. All the mechanisms are cyclic, and the humour lies as much in the order of their reappearance, or the way they are superimposed on each other, as in the way they are mechanically switched on and off. It is as if Birtwistle had decided to say farewell to the priority he had been giving to cyclic processes by treating them lightheartedly. Thereafter he shifted the emphasis from the cyclic to the linear.

Indeed, some of his earlier pieces provide strong hints that this might happen. None more so than *Refrains and Choruses* (1) where the refrains are so varied it is difficult to hear the connection between them. As a result the attention focuses on the unfolding drama of the piece. The works that immediately follow *Carmen Arcadiae Mechanicae Perpetuum*, notably . . . *agm*. . . and the Clarinet Quintet (58), are even more linear in their orientation. The Clarinet Quintet started life as a series of miniature statements based on what Birtwistle calls 'a pentatonic doodle' (the scales C–D–F–G–A–C–D and F–G–A–C–D–F–G–A), but in the end he transformed them into a long continuous line in which they can be no longer distinguished. In our conversations at Lunegarde, he told me that he had attempted to transform the last act of *The Mask of Orpheus* in like manner. The libretto had been written ten years earlier and like the one for *Yan Tan Tethera* it was based on the assumption that Birtwistle's music was cyclic by nature and required a great deal of repetition. In the last act there are over sixty separate 'numbers', most of them continuing cyclic processes initiated in the previous acts. But when he composed the music Birtwistle included a fairly substantial orchestral substructure which is through-composed.

A similar kind of substructure can also be found in *Yan Tan Tethera*. He considered this to be more intuitive and by implication more in keeping with 'the sanctity of the context' than the one in *The Mask of Orpheus*. When I interviewed him he had just written the scene where Hannah grieves for the loss of her children, and the set revolves rapidly through the cycle of the seasons to indicate the passing of the years. The vocal music stretches the principle of varied repetition to the uttermost. Hannah has two refrains, one is the shepherds' charm which Alan had taught her:

Yan, Tan, Tethera
One-two-three
Sweet Trinity
Keep
Me and my sheep.

The other is the counting of the passing years: 'I grieve for my twins one year underground', the 'one' being replaced by two, three, four, five, six and seven in the subsequent repetitions. After each of these refrains, the chorus of Cheviot sheep echo the number she has got to by using the northern way of counting.

'Now what I've done for the first time is this,' said Birtwistle: 'on one level the music repeats, but on another there's a long – how can I describe it? – a long organic, fugue-like texture in the orchestra which goes right through the section then blossoms into a chorale when the counting reaches the magic number seven. So I have a strophic superstructure as foreground and an organic substructure as background which are independent, or largely independent, of each other.'

Still Movement (64), the string piece he composed immediately after *Yan Tan Tethera*, takes the linear process one step further. The work has a relentless, percussive quality quite unlike any other music composed for strings. It contains divisions, and as often as not these are marked by the reappearance in some form or other of the rhythm that begins the work, yet their purpose is to define the start of the next surge forward rather than the beginning of a new cycle. However, the feature that really distinguishes the work from most of Birtwistle's earlier music is the way a heavily emphasized D near the beginning of the piece becomes increasingly prevalent until eventually it assumes the function of a harmonic goal. This sense of where the music is leading, however, is held back until the coda. Before then it pushes forward in a linear progression suggesting a state of 'becoming' that has no aim other than to strive. The serenity of the *Trois Gymnopédies* has been left far behind.

CANTUS AND CONTINUUM

Birtwistle had already selected the title *Still Movement* before I interviewed him in December 1983, and he knew it would be based on the pastorals in *Yan Tan Tethera*. There are three of these. They cover the time needed for one of the hills to recede into the background as they revolve and the other to come into the foreground. The music consists of textures which oscillate gently within their own orbits, and therefore conform to what Birtwistle means by a 'varied ostinato'. This one comes from the second pastorale when Shepherd Alan comes into the foreground. I have selected it because, although not for strings, it gives a clearer idea of the character of these varied ostinatos than the other two where strings predominate. The upper layer is played by flute, oboe and cor anglais, the middle one by harp, and the lower one by bassoons and horn.

During our conversations, Birtwistle said that varied ostinato was at the root of his music. This is certainly true of the music he was composing at the time and everything he has written since, but it is difficult to find much evidence for it in his earlier music. It only began to become a feature of his style in the seventies when he used varied ostinatos to accompany and set in relief an unfolding lyrical line. A particularly vivid example occurs in the closing few minutes of *Silbury Air.* This is also their principal function in *Still Movement*, except that here the lyrical lines are somewhat etiolated. But in *Secret Theatre* (65), his next work, he based the whole piece on the dramatic relationship of an unfolding line and a series of ostinatos. For these he used the terms *cantus* and *continuum*.

The work was commissioned by the London Sinfonietta for his fiftieth birthday concert which took place in October 1984, three months after his actual birthday on 15 July. In the programme book he published extracts from the 66 pages of random jottings he had made prior to writing the work. They are unique because at no other time has he revealed his inner thoughts about how he works out the first stage of his compositional procedure. Unfortunately he disclosed only a few of his musings and as the jottings seem to have disappeared we may never be privy to their contents in full.

The work is scored for string quintet, wind quintet, trumpet, trombone, piano and percussion, and the extracts begin with his thoughts on how to balance such an ensemble.

First things – instrumentation – instrumentation of London Sinfonietta, remember that Schoenberg's Chamber Symphony sounds overscored in chamber version (underscored in orchestral version). – No real bass, single strings versus centre register winds. Imbalance between single strings and brass. Back of the head ideas can become foreground material by committing them to paper no matter how crude. – Basic idea (not back of head) – music which is divided into two of its most basic elements vertical/horizontal, or melody/accompaniment – not good analogy as it suggests one element, – melody of course being more important than the accompaniment ... divide the ensemble maybe in performance (nothing antiphonal) – ... *important*. Maybe the instruments that make up the horizontal element could change during the performance (beware, not too much coming and going) – maybe they could *stand*? Perhaps? – The two parts (element) need not have a direct one to one relationship. More like two beings in the same labyrinth (not lost I hope) ... MELODY/ACCOMPANI-MENT ... bad analogy, suggesting one more important than the other... CANTUS/CONTINUUM – better way to think – a bit academic maybe – *important* – think, explore notion – FOREGROUND/BACKGROUND (juxtaposition of opposites again). Foreground must not always be assigned to CANTUS – *question* if there is a FORE-GROUND/BACKGROUND what would be the MIDDLE-GROUND? think about this ... thought ... a brain moves forward ... If the CANTUS is made or performed by more than one instrument and must not be in any way contra-puntal, then it will consist of several instruments speaking as a single voice (choral unison). Make list of types of unison later ... Individual *single* voices (single instru-ments) could play in the CONTINUUM reducing the CANTUS from maybe, FOREGROUND to MIDDLE-GROUND – think about this.

'Even as I scribble the idea of the CANTUS seems to be the primary consideration (must fight this) – It must not be reduced to a constant role of background. Each of their journeys must be as eventful as the other. List of unisons ... *Ostinato* list A – link with CONTINUUM (important) – important why? Maybe obvious but state it clearly. CON-TINUUM equals vertical music (rhythmic development) CANTUS equals horizontal music (melodic development) CONTINUUM to be made up from invented ostinato forms, plus solos. *Question* – at what point does an ostinato cease to function as such, due to the number of notes present in it? or the amount of time for it to register as a repeat – Why mention this? – Ostinato into melody perhaps – Examine, work out, remember, working procedures for invented ostinatos, – contrapuntal ostinatos etc. – Having done this, hide it or lose it so that it won't be precompositional ... Things becoming a little clearer, but one area mentioned before cannot be left – if the instruments of the CANTUS are going to change during the course of the piece, and there are to be solos in the CONTINUUM then some sort of instrumental role playing is implied – this is interesting. The role playing could move on a totally different plane to that of the ideas of FOREGROUND/ MIDDLEGROUND/BACKGROUND, a sort of independent strata (this is more than just interesting) – *important* do not precompose the idea of ROLE PLAYING, let any logic in that direction come out of the composed context – it should make a sort of hidden drama on an independent level ... Like a secret theatre ...'

Later Birtwistle came across Robert Graves's poem 'Secret Theatre' and quoted the first stanza and the first three lines of the third and last stanza at the top of his score. They are relevant not only to the music, but also to the dedication of the work to his wife who was formerly a dancer.

> When from your sleepy mind the day's burden
> Falls like a bushel sack on a barn floor,
> Be prepared for music, for natural mirages
> And for night's incomparable parade of colour.
>
> . . . .
>
> It is hours past midnight now; a flute signals
> Far off; we mount the stage as though at random,
> Boldly ring down the curtain, then dance out our
> love ...

When playing the *continuum* the instrumentalists sit in a semi-circle facing the conductor; when playing the *cantus* they stand facing the conductor on the left-hand side of the platform behind the *continuum*. The *cantus* instruments are flute, oboe, clarinet, horn, trumpet and the two violins – in other words those that are portable.

Birtwistle had first used the term *cantus* for the melodic line in *Entr'actes and Sappho Fragments* (11), where it is performed by a soprano and flute standing at opposite ends of the platform with the accompanying instruments sitting in a semi-circle between them. In the last song the soprano and flute share the same line; on some occasions the flute supplies a simultaneous variation of the vocal line to produce various types of heterophony, on others it ornaments it either at the same pitch or in free *organum*. The melodic line in *Secret Theatre*, on the other hand, can be presented in up to five or six different ways simultaneously. Yet even when the texture is at its densest the heterophony is never as complex as in the earlier work.

The word *continuum* first appeared in the second act of *The Mask of Orpheus* where it is used to describe the sound of Orpheus's lyre fluctuating in the background as if heard in a dream. It comes from five plucked instruments playing the notes of a single chord over and over again in differing rhythmical ostinatos. Later in *Silbury Air* and the third act of *The Mask of Orpheus*, Birtwistle also used the word for ostinatos going on 'continuously' in the background. But in *Secret Theatre* the ostinatos have a dramatic function and are frequently placed in the foreground. Being essentially rhythmic in nature the emphasis they receive means that for most of the time the music is dance-like and intensely alive. Listeners may find it hard to believe that Robert Graves's injunction to 'boldly ring down the curtain, then dance out our love' was not in Birtwistle's mind from the beginning. The only time he abandons ostinatos is in the hushed and mysterious passage at the end of the fourth section, when the piano and tam-tams take over before the long build-up to the final climax.

As he makes clear in his jottings, the purpose of the piece is that *cantus* and *continuum* should interact dramatically. Birtwistle's favourite dramatic procedure in his instrumental music involves an exchange of roles. An excellent example can be found in *Verses* for clarinet and piano (15), where the piano's flamboyance and the clarinet's extremely controlled character are exchanged in a canon when the two partners behave in more or less exactly the same way. *Secret Theatre*, however, is five times longer than *Verses* so the change from melody into *ostinato* in the *cantus*, and from ostinato into melody in the *continuum*, needs to take place several times rather than once. The transformations in the *cantus* usually occur when the line becomes so elaborate that it loses its identity as a melody and breaks up into repetitive units. In the *continuum*, the process is reversed. The ostinatos become more varied and gradually take on a lyrical character. On occasions, however, melodies appear in the *continuum* without any preparation. A case in point is the appearance of the bassoon at the beginning of the slow, third section of the work (figure 23). It follows a scherzo-like section where the *cantus* instruments end up by playing such a vigorous and insistent texture that only a clean break can bring it to an end. In this context, the return to something melodious has to come from the accompanying instruments. During the course of the bassoon's melody the *cantus* instruments move into the middleground and 'shadow' it. Later when they return to the foreground with a lyrical melody of their own, the bassoon forgoes its prominence.

When he was musing about the problems of scoring in his jottings, Birtwistle referred to Schoenberg's First Chamber Symphony. Perhaps it is not without significance that, like the Chamber Symphony, *Secret Theatre* is also cast in one continuous movement divided into five sections. Schoenberg's score contains an exposition, a scherzo, a development section, a slow movement and a finale where the exposition is recapitulated. In other words it combines sonata form with elements of a four-movement symphony. Birtwistle, however, has an aversion to sonata form and the symphony, and had to find another method of construction. He retained the scherzo and slow movement, but turned the first, fourth and fifth sections into less formal and more dramatic climactic structures. These build up in stages to a culminating point and then wind down to a moment of repose. Although they have their origin in nineteenth-century music, Birtwistle's climactic structures have none of the romantic associations formerly attached to them. For him they are the best means of giving shape to a linear process that has to be brought to a conclusion.

The character of these five sections is determined by the role-playing Birtwistle talked about in his jottings. The scherzo, for instance, takes its character from the role the trombone assumes throughout its course – that of a buffoon. It establishes this character by its glissandos and raspberry-blowing even before the section starts, and eventually it leads the ensemble into a grotesque dance. The slow movement, on the other hand, takes its character from the plaintive role selected for the bassoon. Instrumental role-playing has always been an essential part of Birtwistle's style. In a sense he treats his players as actors. As well as establishing character, role-playing has a dramatic function. This is already evident in *Refrains and Choruses* where the horn as the only brass instrument in the wind quintet plays the role of the disruptive odd-man-out when the music arrives at the perfectly symmetric chord discussed earlier.

Birtwistle said that the role-playing in *Secret Theatre* could make 'a sort of hidden drama on an independent level'. By this I think he meant that the character he had selected for certain instruments determined how they played in the background before being exposed in the middleground or foreground. The trombone's glissandos, for instance, are present in the first section, but in that context they are hardly noticeable. In the course of composing the work, however, the role-playing of individual instruments, although important in the early stages of the piece, gradually gives way to the even more dramatic role-playing Birtwistle provides for the instruments playing collectively as a group.

The section in which the role-playing of an individual instrument has the most decisive influence on the drama is the first. As might be expected after reading Robert Graves's poem, it is the flute that leads the dance. The work opens with it moving from the *continuum* to the *cantus* position, then playing a lilting melody that gradually changes its character after the oboe and clarinet join the *cantus*. It moves back to the *continuum* when the melody has completely lost its flute-like character and becomes rhetorical and impassioned. From its position in the *continuum*, the flute takes up the short, rapid, bird-like gestures that have begun to appear in the *cantus*, gradually smoothing them out to make a brilliant running melody. It is this that sweeps the music to its climax. At this point the flute drops out leaving the *cantus* and *continuum* to confront each other in a series of violent, antiphonal exchanges. On its return, it assumes the role of a calming agent, gently manoeuvring the music into a state of stillness. The situation is then ripe for the contrasting scherzo where the trombone becomes dominant.

The fourth and fifth sections (starting at figures 31 and 43 respectively) are much longer than the first three, and it is here that collective role-playing becomes decisive. The fifth contains the most dramatic build-up in the whole work. Its climax is marked by the entry of the crotales, sounding like a peal of bells. To produce the necessary excitement for the arrival of this epiphany, Birtwistle repeats over and over again a two-note figure the violins and viola played at the very beginning of the work. The notes are the D and F above middle C. In this context, apart from building up tension, they have two more functions: one is as a motif recapitulated to bring the music back to its starting point, the other as a harmony that needs to be resolved. In fact, the repetition of D and F on the viola constitutes the last ostinato in the work. Against it the double bass descends to a low C, and for the first time in the work we are given a note which feels utterly stable.

This resolution on to C, a note that has not been particularly prominent in the work, represents a typically modal solution to the harmony. Compared to those in tonal music, the poles of attraction in modal music are relatively weak so that the initial harmonic centre need not be paramount; it can change. At the beginning of the work, E is the pole of attraction. It may not be particularly strong, but nevertheless it exerts an influence over events. Unfortunately the first page (or pages) of the sketches in the British Library is missing so it has to be assumed that the initial symmetrical arrangement of the notes used by the strings playing the *continuum* was an eleven-note chromatic scale which had E as its axis of symmetry. From this Birtwistle selected six notes for the cello and six for the double bass.

His re-ordering and redistribution of these two groups of six notes appears at the top of page 2 of the sketches.

From these he constructs the ostinato that the cello and double bass contribute to. The double bass plays an octave lower so that its B, the dominant of E, is the lowest note. In this context the D/F motif played repeatedly by the violins and viola represents the neighbour notes of E in the Phrygian mode. The flute, on the other hand, draws its melody from the first four and the last four notes of the standard wedge-shape pattern starting on E.

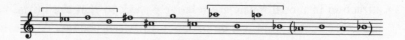

By reshuffling these two groups of four notes to make four groups, Birtwistle constructs a highly coherent line consisting of three versions of E-E♭-F-D and one of A♭-B-A-B♭.

Interlocking three- or four-note units in this manner is a characteristic feature of Birtwistle's technique. It means that a line can be made out of a single motif. Since the sketches for this flute melody must have been on the missing first page, we have to assume he composed the lilting rhythm intuitively.

A quaver after the flute plays that last note, the harmony is focused by the entrance of the horn playing a single stopped E. Nevertheless it must be stressed that the harmony is never as simple as this again. Within a short while it begins to become

much more ambiguous. The sketches indicate that at every juncture Birtwistle works out the details of what he has in mind in
ways appropriate to the context. On the whole, symmetric formations tend to predominate. Nevertheless modal implications are
never lost sight of, and at certain key moments, such as at or near
the end of sections, they come into the foreground. Just before
the *cantus* and *continuum* have their aggressive exchanges near the
end of the first section, for instance, the *cantus* instruments have
a simple, evenly paced line which incorporates the D/F motif and
cadences quite firmly on D.

Although it does not exert a strong gravitational pull until
halfway through the last section, from this moment on, D is the
pitch to which the music tends to return. The harmony has ultimately to resolve on to C because the constant repetition of D
renders it increasingly unstable on the grounds that repetition
creates the expectation of change.

Birtwistle regards *Secret Theatre* as a key work in his output.
He equates it with *Verses for Ensembles* (25), the work that
brought the sectional style he adopted for *Punch and Judy* to
such a forthright and unequivocal culmination in the late
sixties. He believes that both works sum up a particular way of
proceeding. But whereas *Verses for Ensembles* stands at the end of
a line, *Secret Theatre* is the vanguard of a long series of works
that have continued to explore the relationship between *cantus*
and *continuum*. Among other things, the clear difference
between melody and accompaniment opened up his return to
song writing.

SONGS BY MYSELF

Although he had composed a solo cantata and dramatic scenes such as *Ring a Dumb Carillon* (12) and *Nenia* (34), Birtwistle had not written any lyrical songs since *Entr'actes and Sappho Fragments* (11) in 1964. But as soon as he completed *Secret Theatre* he composed a set of five to words he himself had written some eighteen months earlier. They were given under his own direction at his fiftieth birthday concert along with *Secret Theatre*. Since then he has produced nineteen more, the most recent being the six he composed in 1995 for *Pulse Shadows* (101), the longest and most wide-ranging of all his concert works.

He claims he has always had difficulty in finding suitable texts for songs. Those he selected for *Entr'actes and Sappho Fragments* suggest that they have to be elliptical, paradoxical and contain a fairly high degree of melancholy. Ideally he needs a text that reflects his musical preoccupations and contains an image that can be represented in music. In this respect his songs resemble those of Schubert or Britten, for like them he tends to focus on one particular musical image in the course of them. The four songs in *Entr'actes and Sappho Fragments* have musical images which are variants of the same figure so that they help to unify the work. The figure in question is a rapid, tapping rhythm on a single note first introduced by the flute at the end of the third, purely instrumental entr'acte. Its transformations in the songs convey successively stabbing pain, quivering leaves, the fluttering of a lonely woman's heart, and finally the trampling of wild hyacinths under the feet of passing shepherds.

Songs by Myself (66), the five songs he composed in 1984, are based on words he says were dredged from the silt of his subconscious during a spate of holiday melancholy on an island in the southern Dodecanese in the spring of the previous year.

I

O light set a flame in amber, and freeze
the rose's pulse.

II

I lean against a shade, cold thoughts,
so warm your heavy lids with still
shrouded dreams.
This wind which caught me leaving,
becalmed its own shyness ... so twist
its keen direction towards a final end.

III

Cold statements thaw time's stillness,
but once the daydream's midnight
belled slow refrain ends, – listlessly
dipping my finger in the petrified waters of
its daytime ring, I move the fretting pulse
of yesterday's tomorrow.

IV

Steps; bequeathed entrances, falling
below a line of shore ... lie still,
move your eyes, let this vision of time
declare itself void.

V

This silence before light cuts a knot
of dreams
1 – 2 2 – 1 1 – 2 2 – 1 ...
glass framed shadows from blue
circles
stops my breath.

Birtwistle makes no physical distinction between *cantus* and
continuum in *Songs by Myself*; he therefore has no need to label
them as such. As in *Entr'actes and Sappho Fragments* the *cantus* is
shared by soprano and flute (in this instance doubling alto flute),
but in this work the accompanying instruments are vibraphone,
piano, violin, viola, cello and double bass.

The advantage for a composer in setting his own words is that he knows what lies behind the images. In this instance they reflect his musical preoccupation with movement and stillness. The work is therefore closely related to the string piece he composed earlier in the year; indeed in the second song he quotes the opening of *Still Movement*. The work is structured so that the moment of greatest stillness lies at the centre, the third song. Here the accompaniment, built entirely from ostinatos oscillating quietly within their own orbits without any change of harmony, creates the impression that movement is taking place only on the surface and at the deepest level the song is actually motionless. The other songs are concerned with events in which movement is transformed into stillness. In the first the musical image for light being set in amber and the pulse of the rose becoming frozen is a bell-like sound rapidly fading into silence. And in the second, where the words 'shade,' 'shrouded' and 'final end' suggest a movement towards death, Birtwistle uses the opening of *Still Movement* to suggest the halting steps of an old man.

The prevailing musical image in the fourth song comes from the words 'lie still, move your eyes'. The strings, playing inter- mittently an unchanging chord, represent the stillness, while the flute and piano indulging in rapid *fioriture* represent the move- ment. But before the soprano sings 'void' all movement stops. In the final song the piano has even more elaborate arabesques. They are set against a melodic line shared by the soprano and flute, and an intermittent, very tight staccato figure played by the viola. It is this figure which the soprano uses for 'Stops my breath'. As in the first two songs, movement has given way to stillness, but these last two confirm that it is the ultimate stillness which is being sought.

Apart from when the soprano takes over a figure which had previously belonged to the *continuum* at the very end of the last song, the relationship between *cantus* and *continuum* in *Songs by Myself* is fairly traditional. The soprano and flute have the melody, the other instruments the accompaniment. However in *Words Overheard* (68), the song he composed for soprano and chamber orchestra to his own words in 1985, the relationship is much closer to the one in *Secret Theatre*. The text is fragmentary – snippets of a monologue or conversation overheard without any knowledge of context. Once again the topic is time and the juxtaposition of movement and stillness. For example: 'the moon's still realm moves ... again again and again ...' But for this song he devised the text so that the soprano as well as having the cantus can also adopt the characteristics of the *continuum*. In these instances she sings ostinatos in which the emphasis is on rhythm rather than melody. To highlight the contrast between her two roles, Birtwistle uses *melisma* for the *cantus* and a syllabic style for the *continuum*. To justify the use of several notes to a syllable at the start of the work, he opens poetically: 'A song's slow numbers lie beneath this night's cold wraps ... sing ... sing again again again and a gain a ...' The style becomes syllabic when the words become more conversational and matter-of-fact in the central section: 'at this time ... she would smile ... and on that day ... when we had met ...' In this song there is no need for a descriptive musical image because in a sense the words are the music. They reflect both its nature and the structure Birtwistle had in mind for the piece. For instance, to round it off he places the melismatic and syllabic styles in close proximity, using three notes for the two syllables of the last 'again': 'that day she would forget the sky ... but like I would one day ... when I ... say ... she ... again ...' The meaning may be ambiguous, but the stress on 'again', coming as it does after being sung so exultantly at the end of the first section, gives the song a life-enhancing quality which in some way compensates for the gloom hanging over *Songs by Myself.* It is also a pointer to the way he will end many of the works that are to follow.

EARTH DANCES

Most of 1985 was devoted to the composition of the orchestral work the BBC had commissioned for its Symphony Orchestra, and had scheduled for performance in March 1986. It was to be his first major work for orchestra since the completion of *The Triumph of Time* thirteen years earlier. Most of his admirers consider *The Triumph of Time* to be one of his finest works, and he now shares this opinion. But in the years following its first performance, including the time when he was composing the new piece, he looked on it with a certain amount of disapproval. In my conversations with him it was difficult to pinpoint why this should be. All he would say was that the continuity was not to his liking, and that it was 'the kind of piece they expected an avant-garde composer to write at the time'. By this I presumed he meant that he thought its outcome was too predictable.

All his works for symphony orchestra are cast in one long continuous movement and structured so as to gradually bring into the foreground something that had originally been in the background. In *Chorales* (7) the process involves the gradual stripping away of the proliferations which obscure the chorales lying beneath the surface at the beginning. In *Nomos* (22), it is the gradual emergence into prominence of a *cantus firmus* played by four amplified wind instruments. While in *An Imaginary Landscape* (38) the main interest lies in a chorale which, when fully revealed, turns out to be a deeply sombre valediction.

This is the strategy that lies behind *The Triumph of Time*, but in this work the process leads to the idea being degraded rather than enhanced. Birtwistle had two shots at writing the piece. The first begins with a lyrical melody for soprano saxophone which gradually breaks away from its accompaniment by proceeding in a tempo of its own. But as the orchestra's texture gets fuller, the saxophone's confidence begins to crumble. It is reduced to playing over and over again first a phrase of three notes then a phrase of two notes directed to be played 'as if screaming'. But the degradation had come too soon, and so Birtwistle abandoned the project. It was at this stage, perhaps even before, that he came across Brueghel's engraving and the idea of a procession of unrelated musical objects came into his head, the three-note saxophone phrase becoming the feature that will eventually come into its own when it turns into a 'screamed out' chorale at the climax of the work. I believe it was this he considered too predictable, and as a consequence he wanted to avoid being so obvious in his next work for orchestra.

His programme note for the first performance of *Earth Dances* (69), the new piece, says that when writing the work he likened himself to 'a traveller in a big city who moves around seeing familiar landmarks in different contexts and perspectives, and gradually building up an idea of the city as a whole, although he can never grasp the entire plan in a single view'. Later he said that it is like 'a giant labyrinth, whose formal units appear nearly identical, but wherever you are inside it, whichever corner you turn, there is some new aspect or perspective'. Neither of these statements suggests that the work has something that will move from background to foreground during its course, as his previous orchestral works had done. All that can be said is that the sole purpose of entering a labyrinth is to find one's way out.

Birtwistle called the work *Earth Dances* mainly because he cast the material in layers which could be compared to the strata in a rock face such as a cliff. But in selecting the title, I think he also had in mind *The Rite of Spring,* where as often as not the material is also placed in layers piled up on top of each other. Indeed in the second part of *Earth Dances*, the build-up to the climax contains passages reminiscent of the way Stravinsky builds up tension in the 'Dance of the Earth' and 'Sacrificial Dance'.

Birtwistle is deeply indebted to Stravinsky's score. Among other things, it gave him the idea that he too could invent an ancient world, in particular the mystery, the 'no-holds-barred' violence and sensuality of ancient, pre-Socratic Greece. But in this new work, the obsessive ostinatos in the second part suggest that he may have had an even more archaic world in mind.

The precedent for placing the material in layers can be found in . . . *agm* . . ., the big choral work he scored for sixteen voices and three instrumental groups: eleven high instruments, nine low instruments, and various punctuating instruments (piano, harps and percussion). The voices and the high and low instruments define the horizontal layers, the punctuating instruments the vertical layer. In my first book I selected a passage from about a quarter of the way through to point out that the horizontal layers in any one passage are variations of the same line. In *Earth Dances* the layers are more independent of each other. The three most important, those lying in the lower, middle and upper parts of the total spectrum of six octaves, are each defined by their own hierarchy of intervals. In the lower register the most prominent are fourths and fifths. The simplest example is a passage for two tubas near the end of the work. To make it easier to read I have transposed their music up an octave.

The most prominent intervals in the middle register are thirds, particularly minor thirds. The first minor third in this passage from near the beginning of the work is the D/F motif. Later on it will receive even greater prominence than in *Secret Theatre*.

In the upper register he gives prominence to wide intervals: sixths, sevenths and ninths.

The problem for the listener is that the material is constantly developing and the layers frequently overlap. On several occasions the characteristic material of one layer 'migrates' to another, and has to return to the one it has come from by means of a scale or 'ladder'. For instance, when the tubas play their organum-like harmony quoted above, the upper woodwind have a high line composed of a rising semitone and minor third, i.e. intervals associated with the middle register. To return these to where they belong, the flute rapidly descends via a two-octave scale down to the D above middle C. When it reaches its destination, the violins take over, inverting the pattern the woodwind have played so that it becomes a falling semitone and minor third. Shorter ladders also link intervals within a layer. The one that functions as a landmark throughout the work is a scale connecting a diminished fifth lying at the top of the lower register.

There are occasions in the second half of the work when these three main layers are divided into as many as six. Birtwistle has then to call on textures as well as intervals to differentiate them. As in his previous three works, the principal textures are those of *cantus* and *continuum*. In one instance the trumpets and horns have a dense cantus-like texture in the upper middle range while above and below them are five layers of mainly rhythmical ostinatos. A symphony orchestra contains choirs of instruments, which means that the relationships between them have to be expressed in much broader gestures than the relationships in a relatively small ensemble of soloists. This means that in *Earth Dances* the metamorphosis of *cantus* into *continuum* and vice versa takes place over a longer period of time and is less dramatic than in *Secret Theatre*. In the first half of the work the *cantus* holds sway, in the second the *continuum*. The *cantus* usually lies in the middle register where the intervals are narrower and much more 'singable' than those in the lower or upper. Although there is no physical distinction between *cantus* and *continuum*, there are two fairly substantial sections in the first half where those instruments playing the melody are grouped together in the score. The first occurs after an introductory section establishing the scale and essential nature of the work. It begins with the D-centred phrase quoted above to represent the intervals in the middle register. After a while this simple melody divides into heterophony and then ascends into the upper register via a scalic ladder. Gradually, as its intervals widen, it becomes increasingly more ornate and finally transforms into an ostinato – at which point another scalic ladder takes it away into the stratosphere! But the purpose behind this theatrical gesture is to prepare the listener for a deeply mysterious section in which the layering can be heard at its clearest. It follows the return of the *cantus* to the middle register after a dance-like episode.

At the centre of the texture lies the slow-moving *cantus* divided into fifteen lines of heterophony played on eight wind instruments, ten violins, five violas and five cellos. This is 'shadowed' in the upper register by a group of high wind instruments, and in the lower register by trombones, tubas and double basses with their characteristic fourths and fifths. In addition to these there are two vertical layers, one a series of widely spread, harmonically dense chords played intermittently by the rest of the strings, the other a sharply etched, essentially rhythmic series of chords played by trumpets, xylophones and various unpitched percussion instruments. The passage reaches its conclusion when the instruments in the upper register begin to become more assertive and eventually descend via a scalic ladder to the middle register where the xylophones take over and pound out the notes D–F–C♯ in preparation for the much more violent events that are to take place in the second half of the work.

By virtue of the fact that these three notes contain the D/F motif, we are provided with the clue as to how the work might end. In this respect the work is very similar to *Secret Theatre*, because the motif becomes prominent in the build-up to the final climax and ultimately resolves on to a low C in the double basses. There are, however, two fundamental differences. One is that in *Secret Theatre* the note D is only fleetingly dwelt on in the first half of the work, whereas in *Earth Dances* it returns so frequently that even before the xylophones pound out those three notes it has become an important point of reference. The other is that just before the resolution on to C, the horns, trombones and tubas sustain a long G which grows from *piano* to triple *forte* and becomes increasingly like a dominant. The impression is confirmed when the basses slip quietly down to C and a strong sense of arrival is achieved. In retrospect it can be seen that as in Birtwistle's previous orchestral works an event initially lying in the background has ultimately been brought to the foreground. But it is only near the end that the function of D as a potential supertonic is revealed. And it is only then that the way out of the labyrinth comes into view.

Neither before nor since has Birtwistle been so traditional in his use of long-range harmony. Nevertheless, *Earth Dances* marks a turning point in the way he brings works to a conclusion. He has always prided himself on his codas. Previously, when cyclic processes were so important to him, he tended to let the music drift away as if it were continuing out of earshot. A prime example occurs in *Medusa* (31) where the music takes nearly five minutes to fade away. The only occasions when he felt it necessary to end conclusively were in pieces such as *Tragoedia* (14) and *Verses for Ensembles* (25), which set out to be bold public statements. In his recent works, this has tended to be the norm even in intimate pieces.

Meanwhile the nature of Birtwistle's 'bold statements' has also changed with and after *Earth Dances*. For this is the first of his blockbusters. *Tragoedia* and *Verses for Ensembles* are divided into sections with gaps between them, whereas *Earth Dances* never lets up during its nearly forty minutes' duration. Even though it contains passages of deep stillness and mystery, it nevertheless takes the listener by storm. When he had almost completed the score he heard about the death of Brigitte Schiffer, the critic and writer on contemporary music to whom he had dedicated *Words Overheard*. Under one bar, just after the repetitions of the D/F motif begin to make an impact in the second half of the work, he writes 'RIP B.S'. Ideally the bar should have been a silent one. But there are no silent bars in the score. The work allows no time for reflection. The one Birtwistle chose contains two notes held by trombones, tubas and double basses. Nothing actually 'happens' in it, but it is over in a flash.

Two months after its highly successful première, English National Opera produced *The Mask of Orpheus* at the London Coliseum. Michael Tippett, who attended the first performance, said he was 'totally shattered by the tremendous work'. 'I was writing *New Year* at the time,' he wrote later, 'and had to stop, take a breath and consider what lessons I might learn from it. As things turned out, I was not 'influenced', but I could only marvel at the way it (and everyone involved in it) so courageously, so tenaciously regenerated an art-form often regarded these days as dead.* Alfred Brendel was even more enthusiastic. He called it 'the first English masterpiece for 300 years'.

It had taken Birtwistle sixteen years to write the opera and get it staged. Initially he and his librettist, Peter Zinovieff, had toyed with basing the work on the Faust legend, but the range of its versions and interpretations could not compare with those the Orpheus story had inspired. To stage an opera which presents a story from so many different angles requires a cyclic structure rather than the linear one usually adopted for unfolding a plot on stage. The authors had therefore to borrow techniques from other media, especially those where it was possible to be highly stylized: one was mime, another the puppet theatre. It was from these that Birtwistle and Zinovieff had the idea of duplicating the roles of the principal characters by having a mime represent Orpheus, Euridice and Aristaeus as hero or heroine, and a puppet to represent them as myth. But the most extensive borrowing came from the cinema, for as well as employing accelerated and slow motion, the opera also makes extensive use of cutting, flash-backs and flash-forwards. In addition to this, each act is governed by a formal structure which has its own rules and is mainly inde-pendent of the action.

The opera had originally been commissioned in 1970 by Covent Garden, but by 1975, after it had been passed on to Glyndebourne, it had to be abandoned. Both institutions were keen to promote a major work by Birtwistle, but had reluctantly come to the conclusion that it would be too expensive to mount. Zinovieff's original libretto fills four fat volumes, and reads like a film director's highly detailed shooting script. With no prospect of a production in view, Birtwistle put the score into cold store when he was near the end of Act Two. Work was resumed when English National Opera renewed the commission

* Sir Michael Tippett, *Those Twentieth Century Blues*, London 1991, p.225.

in the early eighties. It meant that as well as completing the second act and writing the third, he had also to compose the extensive electronic components the work demanded. For this he was assisted by the New Zealand composer, Barry Anderson, who laboured in the studios of IRCAM in Paris virtually day and night for two years to produce the results Birtwistle required.

Given the complexity of the opera, it was almost inevitable the director would find it difficult to meet some of its demands. David Freeman had been chosen for the task because he had directed Opera Factory in a stunning production of *Punch and Judy* at London's Action Space in 1982. On the whole he succeeded in overcoming many of the problems, but it did mean simplifying the set and accepting the fact that British opera singers and mime artists are not trained to be as stylized in their acting as Birtwistle and Zinovieff required. They were therefore allowed to be more naturalistic than had been intended. However, there are six episodes in the opera where stylization is absolutely crucial. These are the six interludes of mime and electronic music which when they happen 'freeze' whatever is going on in the orchestra or on stage. They tell the stories that Orpheus told to the trees and rocks after he has lost Euridice for a second time, and have to be performed by a group of mime actors at such a breakneck speed that everything following will appear to be in slow motion even though it is not. When the opera was given a semi-staged performance by the BBC during the Secret Theatres Festival in 1996, the combined efforts of The Cholmondelys and The Featherstonehaughs under the direction of the choreographer Lea Anderson achieved the desired effect. They made it clear that the things that Birtwistle and Zinovieff requested that had once seemed impractical are now well within the bounds of possibility.

Six weeks after *The Mask of Orpheus* finished its run at the London Coliseum, *Yan Tan Tethera* had its première in the Queen Elizabeth Hall. Although the work had been commissioned jointly by Radio 3 and BBC 2, the money for its commission had come from Radio 3, and it was they who had to take the initiative when BBC 2 became undecided about whether to proceed with a studio production or not. After much internal debate, Radio 3 received approval from the BBC's governors to approach Channel 4. Meanwhile permission had been given to Opera Factory/London Sinfonietta to mount a staged production in the Queen Elizabeth Hall as part of the 1986 Summerscope Festival. Instead of recording a production of its own, Channel 4 decided to give Opera Factory financial assistance and to record David Freeman's stage version. It was televised the following year as part of a series of programmes which included *Punch and Judy*, *Down by the Greenwood Side* and a documentary about Birtwistle called *Behind the Mask*. As a result *Yan Tan Tethera* has never received a studio production, and now that television opera is a thing of the past, it is unlikely to have one in the future.

A stage performance is perfectly feasible and indeed Birtwistle always had this possibility in mind. But ideally the work needs three revolves and the Queen Elizabeth Hall is not a theatre and consequently lacks such facilities. It was therefore impossible to have the set look like 'a big clock mechanism, like one of those intricate clocks you get in Bavaria'. Essentially the work belongs to the same genre as *Punch and Judy* and *Down by the Greenwood Side* (27), that is to say dramatic pieces which draw on the highly stylized world of children's theatre. Not only has everything to behave 'mechanically', it also has to have a strong sense of magic. Birtwistle confesses to being fond of *Yan Tan Tethera*, but nevertheless he has not wanted to write anything like it since.

2
1987–1991

During the five years between the production of *Yan Tan Tethera* and the staging of *Gawain* (81), the first work he was unambiguously to call an 'opera', Birtwistle's reputation rose considerably. Official recognition came when the Queen gave him a knighthood for his services to music in her 1988 birthday honours. Two years earlier the French had made him a Chevalier des arts et des lettres and *The Mask of Orpheus* won him the *Evening Standard* Award for Opera. The following year the television series discussed in the previous chapter was mounted by Channel 4. Later in the same year the University of Louisville gave him the prestigious Grawemeyer Award in succession to Lutoslawski and Ligeti. Early in 1988 the BBC devoted the whole of its annual Festival of Twentieth Century Music in the Barbican Centre to his work and in 1991, when *Gawain* was broadcast on Radio 3, he became 'This Week's Composer' as well as being the featured composer in several festivals. For Aldeburgh he wrote *Four Poems by Jaan Kaplinski* (82), and at Vienna's Modern Festival and the Huddersfield Contemporary Music Festival *Gawain's Journey* (83) received its first performances.

Gawain had been commissioned by the Royal Opera House, Covent Garden, in the summer of 1984. It was the Royal Opera that had originally commissioned *The Mask of Orpheus* and this time Birtwistle was determined to avoid the impracticalities that had led the house to withdraw from its production in the early seventies. He decided the new opera would have to be less expensive to mount and easier to produce. Since Covent Garden had a full symphony orchestra under contract, all the players should be employed, not just the wind, harps and percussion. He also felt that a director ought to be appointed to advise the librettist on theatrical matters as soon as the text was under way. In addition he was determined the new opera would not involve electronics. He considered the amount of time and effort needed to produce the tapes for *The Mask of Orpheus* had been excessive. He now believes it undermined Barry Anderson's health and may also have contributed to his early death. But the overriding reason was that, no matter how brilliant pre-recorded electronic music can be, it is essentially artificial. It lacks the spontaneity which allows his music to 'breathe'. This is why he can no longer work in the medium.

The idea that the fourteenth century alliterative romance *Sir Gawain and the Green Knight* would make the basis for an opera had been in his mind ever since 1963, when he used the episode about the turning of the seasons for his choral work, *Narration: A Description of the Passing of a Year* (8). For his librettist he chose David Harsent who had just published *Mister Punch*,* a volume of poetry which treated the outrageous puppet in much the same way Birtwistle had done in *Punch and Judy*. Harsent, however, had taken Punch out of his usual environment and cast him as the grotesque 'shadow' who runs amok in our everyday world rather than in just a puppet theatre. Like Birtwistle's opera, his poems involve a journey of self-discovery, the climax being a series of nightmares which result in Punch finding peace within himself.

Harsent, who had not seen *Punch and Judy* before he wrote the poems, had no hesitation in accepting the invitation to turn the great Middle English alliterative poem into a modern verse drama suitable for an opera, for it he had long admired the romance and found the prospect challenging. The only fundamental change he needed to make was to establish the motivation behind the events at the beginning rather than hold it back until

---

* David Harsent, *Mister Punch*, Oxford 1984.

the end, as happens in the poem. The action takes place in Arthurian times, and what sets everything in motion is the hatred of the enchantress Morgan le Fay for Arthur and Guinevere. To make an effective drama, she has to reveal her intention to 'do them down' from the start. To do this she needs an accomplice to converse with, and this is none other than the person who is to be Gawain's seducer. She is unnamed in the original poem but Harsent calls her Lady de Hautdesert.

The text for the first of the two acts was submitted to Birtwistle when *The Mask of Orpheus* was still in rehearsal. At that stage neither Harsent nor Birtwistle had given much thought as to who the director should be, but later in the year they flew to New York to see whether Peter Sellars might be interested. According to Harsent, Sellars was unsympathetic both to the original poem and what he had written; he would have preferred the leading female characters to be 'goodies' rather than schemers. He therefore proposed that Harsent's libretto be scrapped and replaced by one he would get a friend to write. Since this was out of the question, the director Birtwistle eventually chose was Di Trevis. Her work had been mainly confined to the spoken theatre, but Birtwistle had known her since his days at the National Theatre and was confident that her skill, imagination and musicality would fit the bill, as indeed was the case. However the delay in appointing her, and the time Harsent needed to implement the suggestions she and Birtwistle made, meant that the final libretto was not ready until the spring of 1989, leaving Birtwistle only eighteen months to write the score.

The sketches for it show that apart from passages involving rapid exchange between characters, such as when the members of Arthur's court respond to the Green Knight's challenge ('God's name' – 'You dare' – 'Choose me'), the vocal lines were written before the orchestral accompaniment. This is immediately apparent in the very first scene where the vocal lines for Morgan le Fay and her companion are written out neatly as if they had been composed previously and simply copied. The orchestral part, on the other hand, is often little more than a rough scribble with multiple crossings-out. As one reads through the sketches it soon becomes evident that Birtwistle is endeavouring to make the accompaniment both supportive of the vocal line and yet independent of it.

This tendency to make melody and accompaniment independent of each other is one of his preoccupations between 1987 and 1991. In one of the last works he composed in this period, *An Interrupted Endless Melody* for oboe and piano (85), he took this independence to an extreme. The oboe has the *cantus*, the piano the *continuum*, and it is clear from the sketches for the work that the two parts were written without any reference to each other. There is no score and the players are instructed to make no attempt to co-ordinate with each other. Since Birtwistle supplies the oboist with different versions of the *cantus* and leaves it to the player to select which one to perform, even listeners who have heard the work before may be faced with the unexpected. Ultimately it is they who must find connections between *cantus* and *continuum*. The situation may be highly ambiguous, but in this lies the poetry.

GAWAIN'S LIBRETTO

Although it draws on pagan fertility rites associated with the Green Man, *Sir Gawain and the Green Knight* is essentially a Christian poem incorporating the belief that fallen humanity cannot achieve the perfection of Christ. Yet even though Gawain's courage, good faith, courtesy and chastity may be flawed, he nevertheless brings honour and glory to the House of King Arthur.

The poet divides his 2,530 lines of alliterative verse into four fitts each devoted to a particular aspect of Gawain's qualities as the 'golden boy' of Arthur's Round Table.

FITT 1. Arthur and Guinevere, along with Gawain, Agravain, Ywain, Bishop Baldwin and other members of the court are seated at a New Year's feast in Camelot, but Arthur says he cannot eat until he has witnessed or been told about something extraordinary. As if on cue a huge man dressed in green bearing an axe and a holly bough rides in. He challenges a member of the court to cut off his head if that person will submit himself to him the following year and suffer the same fate. Gawain steps forward and duly severs the Green Knight's head from his body. To everyone's astonishment the decapitated knight picks up his head and rides away. But before leaving he tells Gawain that next year he must journey to a place called the Green Chapel in the north of England where he too will face beheading.

FITT 2. The seasons pass, and on All Souls' Day Gawain is armed by a lamenting court. His journey takes him through Wales and the Wirral, and at every stage he has to suffer severe wintry conditions and the harassment of wild animals, ogres and dragons. Eventually, on Christmas Eve, he comes to a castle where he is graciously received and made welcome by Bertilak, the lord, and his beautiful wife. To amuse themselves over the Christmas period, Bertilak suggests that they play an exchange game. He will go out hunting and when he returns in the evening will present Gawain with whatever he has killed. In exchange Gawain must give him whatever he has gained in the house.

FITT 3. For three consecutive days Bertilak hunts and Gawain, famous for his skill and prowess in love, is amorously approached in his bedroom by the lady of the castle. He manages to resist her advances but permits her to give him a kiss on the first day, two on the second and three on the third. On the third day he also accepts from her a sash which she says will save his life when he wears it. Each evening Gawain exchanges the kisses with his host for the stag, wild boar and fox Bertilak has killed. But on the third evening, when he should have handed over the sash, he breaks the bargain by keeping it for himself.

FITT 4. On New Year's Day, Gawain goes to the Green Chapel, which he discovers to be little more than a mound. There he meets the Green Knight and submits himself to the axe. Three blows are delivered yet none is fatal, the first two miss completely and the last merely nicks his neck. The Green Knight explains that he brought the axe down in a manner that represents Gawain's behaviour when they exchanged their winnings. On all three occasions Gawain delivered the kisses, but on the third he withheld the sash and for this his neck was nicked. A death blow was never intended because the desire to save one's own life is not dishonourable. He then discloses that he is Bertilak transformed into the Green Knight by the magic of Morgan le Fay who wants to undermine the prestige of Arthur's court by revealing that the knights of the Round Table are not as courageous or virtuous as had been assumed. Gawain bitterly curses his failings, but when he returns to Camelot the court consider his exploits have been heroic. The poem ends with the knights adopting the sash as a baldric.

The only character Harsent adds to the ones in the poem is that of the Court Jester or Fool. In his version these fitts are arranged into two acts, but on Birtwistle's suggestion he extended the short episode describing the turning of the seasons at the beginning of the second fitt into an elaborate masque. This ends the first act and makes the overall structure symmetric, for its cyclic events balance the cyclic events in the seduction scene. As a result the design becomes: Court–Beheading–Masque–Journey–Seduction–Beheading–Court. To complete the symmetry, the design's central episode, the journey, is divided into three parts, the first balancing the last. It opens with Morgan having Gawain in thrall and describing to him as he sets out the hardships he must overcome. Then comes a central section in which the orchestra describes in musical terms the actual journey. After this, as Gawain is nearing his destination, Morgan describes the final part of the journey. Interwoven into this are the voices of Bertilak and his wife welcoming him in advance of his arrival.

Birtwistle wanted the turning of the seasons in the masque to be set against an event taking place in 'real' time, and suggested this could be the arming of Gawain by the court on All Souls' Day. As always happens with Birtwistle's librettists, Harsent soon realized that his text would have to match the composer's musical procedures if it was to be of any use to him. To give the composer the opportunity to make use of the layering and inter-locking features which are part and parcel of his style, he constructed the masque by interweaving seven more or less inde-pendent 'voices', some choral, others solo. In the background is an off-stage chorus with the refrain 'and so the world turns'. On stage, but invisible, are Morgan and Lady de Hautdesert provid-ing descriptions of the changing seasons. Intertwined with these Harsent has Bishop Baldwin sing the hymn 'Dies Irae' as well as joining a choir of clerics to perform new settings of the four Marian antiphons: *Alma Redemptoris Mater, Ave Regina, Regina Caeli Laetare and Salve, Regina, Mater Misercordiae*. While these are going on, Baldwin, Ywain, Agravain and the Fool as a semi-chorus present Gawain with his armour piece by piece, Guinevere sings about the 'golden boy' being in love with the journey he is about to undertake, and Gawain dreams about the enemy he plans to dazzle: 'I dreamed my enemy / kneeling before me, his hands / raised like a supplicant's; / I gave him food and drink.'

Harsent's main problem in turning a narrative poem into something suitable for the stage was the creation of dramatic tension. He dealt with it in two ways. One was to incorporate time shifts. By jumping forward into the future he could rouse expectations; by holding up the action at crucial moments in order to go through past events again he could create suspense. He incorporated both these time shifts in the beheading scene in Act One where tension has to be particularly high. The build-up of expectations for the arrival of the Green Knight starts when Arthur is asking for something extraordinary to happen and we are shown on a screen the figure of a knight travelling through a landscape. Later, through the frequent repetitions of this vision, we come to realize this figure is meant to represent Gawain travelling to the Green Chapel in a year's time, but at this juncture it would seem that someone is hurrying towards Camelot in order to fulfil Arthur's request. Later when one of the Fool's riddles is interrupted by a knocking on the door the audience is bound to call this vision to mind. However the knocking is followed by the opening and closing of the door without anyone entering. The audience has to wait some time for the knocking on the door to be repeated and the astonishing figure of the Green Knight to enter. Later, when Gawain is lifting the axe to behead him, the action is suspended to go through the arrival of the Green Knight again. On this occasion the audience is left in suspense. But this time-shift to the past turns out to be the means by which Harsent can look far ahead into the future. He does so through the words he gives to Morgan and Lady de Hautdesert and then to the Fool after the arrival. In this new context the women's words undoubtedly refer to when Gawain will be waiting for the axe to fall in the Green Chapel: 'This is the moment that waited for you / as you journeyed towards it./ This is the moment you carried with you / from the worst dream.' The reference is confirmed by the Fool's riddle that replaces the one he originally delivered. The meaning may be enigmatic but the words indicate that when he has his head on the block Gawain's thoughts will be taken up not only with the axe but the knowledge that he has failed to live up to his ideals: 'Something bolder than vanity, / something darker than shame, / something swifter than pity, / more zealous, more lavish, than fame. / What is it?'

When he came to set the music Birtwistle cut this out and set the riddle the Fool initially posed. The time-shift to the future may have been spoilt and the establishment of the fool as a seer may have gone by the board, but it could be argued that the repetition of the same words at least makes the time-shift backwards more convincing.

Dramatic tension is also created by keeping Morgan on stage throughout the opera and having her provide a running commentary on what is happening. Although she is never visible to anyone on stage except Lady de Hautdesert during the first act, the audience can witness the action through her eyes as well as its own. She has planned everything, knows what is to happen and can relay this knowledge. What she did not anticipate was Bertilak's jealousy during the seduction scene. In the first act she and her accomplice stand aside from the action. Apart from their opening scene and the masque at the end, most of their remarks are addressed to the unhearing Gawain. In the second act, when Morgan is by herself, she involves herself actively with what is going on. Not only does she take Gawain through the journey, she also lulls him to sleep, comments on his acceptance of the kisses and the sash, leads him to the Green Chapel, tempts him to turn back, and when he returns to Arthur's court, calls on him to undertake a fresh journey. At one stage, when Bertilak and his wife are welcoming him she acts as a prompt, reminds them what they have to say. Throughout the whole of this second act we watch her pulling the strings like a puppet master. The tension arises from our knowledge that her intentions are evil.

Yet neither in the poem nor the opera are her intentions realized. She fails to undermine Arthur and Guinevere or the prestige of the court. Indeed, in the opera her scheming may be of benefit to them. Although the poem is religious in character, Harsent changes it into more of a psychological drama in the course of his adaptation. This becomes evident near the end of Act One when Gawain has been armed, the masque is over and the Fool poses yet another riddle: 'Look out of your window; / you might see/ a shadow flowing over the stones in the courtyard./ Who is it?' In Jungian terminology the shadow is the unconscious 'natural' side of a human being. As I made clear in my first book, Birtwistle and his librettists are indebted to Jung.

In *The Mask of Orpheus*; for instance, 'the shadow' is the name given to Aristaeus. We encounter it in dreams but usually consider it too unruly and dangerous to be brought into consciousness. We prefer to show the world a persona that masks what goes on deep inside us. Yet Jung insisted that we have to acknowledge and accept our shadows if we are to become 'whole', and he likened the process to a psychological journey.

The poem also makes a contrast between two different worlds. In medieval literature, the world of nature – wild, uncontrolled and threatening – is frequently compared to the ordered world of the town and court. Gawain encounters the natural world when he comes face to face with the 'Green Man' and has to journey through Wales and the 'badlands' of the Wirral in the depth of winter. The experience is the prelude to the discovery of his vulnerability and his encounter with an inner world that is equally unruly and disturbing. When he returns to Camelot he says: 'Now I'm home again, / sullen, empty-handed, feverish with knowledge / How will I live / in this tyranny of virtue?' This is the moment when his psychological journey begins. Morgan realizes this at the very end of the opera. Before leaving the stage she repeats what the Fool had said about the shadow flowing over the stones in the courtyard, and goes on to say: 'Look in your mirror; / you might see / the image of someone retreating before your face. / Think only of dreams and promises. / Then . . . with a single step . . . your journey starts.'

Harsent believes that when the members of the court see that Gawain has changed from being a beardless boy to a person of substance they will initiate changes within themselves and indeed in the court as an institution. In his hands the story has a social as well as a religious and psychological dimension. This is why, when he talks about his libretto, he places so much empha-sis on the insights of Guinevere and the Fool in the final scene. Guinevere notes that Gawain has become 'more himself' and the Fool that he 'has returned from a journey with nothing familiar about him except his name'. These words echo those of Lady de

Hautdesert when she makes her exit after the seduction scene. Harsent has her fall in love with Gawain and when she is rejected by him she confesses that she is 'twinned with another woman – dingy, wild, deadlocked by knowledge'. Her final words indicate quite clearly what Harsent has in mind for Gawain and all his fellow knights when the action is over: 'One life here is over, / another begins. / Everything's changed / except my face and name.'

ENDLESS PARADE

Almost a year before being asked by Covent Garden to write a new opera, Birtwistle received a commission from Paul Sacher to compose a work for the Zürich Chamber Orchestra. Whereas he knew almost immediately what kind of work the opera should be, he had no clear idea about the orchestral work until Elgar Howarth played him records of the Swedish trumpet player, Håkan Hardenberger, in late 1986. He had not wanted to write a work purely for strings so soon after *Still Movement*, so a piece which offered him the challenge of balancing strings with an instrument considerably more brilliant and domineering than them made an instant appeal. Even at that early stage he felt that the contrast between soloist and orchestra should be simultaneous and the strings should not be given the opportunity to assert themselves in a tutti. This meant that Hardenberger would need the stamina to play a twenty-minute work without resting. Howarth assured him that he had. Later when he was sent a photograph of the trumpeter he realized he had actually found a Gawain-like 'golden boy' to write for. 'He plays like Joshua and looks like the Angel Gabriel' was his response.

Previously his music for soloist and orchestra had been limited to *Melencolia 1* (48), the work he composed in 1976 for clarinet accompanied by two string orchestras and harp. The title refers to Dürer's engraving showing Melancholia as Geometria sitting in deep thought with the tools of her trade lying scattered about her unable to do anything. In the late sixties it became the subject of an essay by Günter Grass called 'Stasis in Progress'. Grass argued that stasis and progress, melancholy and what he called the quest for Utopia, are head and tail of the same coin. The one could change into the other with ease. Taking his cue from this, Birtwistle realized that 'stasis in progress' could easily be transformed into 'progress in stasis'. It would merely involve an exchange of roles. He therefore assigned to the clarinet the role of a melancholic who gradually unfolds a long slow melody as if, following Dürer, its spontaneity had been crippled by thought. The two string orchestras sit on either side of it playing in a much freer manner material based mainly on varied ostinatos. Both orchestras have the same music but play out of phase with each other so that a blurred and hence distant effect is produced. In the early stages of the work their role is mainly supportive. But later they become increasingly independent of the soloist, and without their support the clarinet can no longer sustain its melody and it begins to break up. Eventually when the strings find their destiny in a chorale sixty-two parts thick, the soloist is reduced to the equivalent of a sequence of screams. This proves to be the turning point of the work, for immediately afterwards the strings dissolve their parts in a series of ostinatos that behave like mobiles set in motion by air currents. When the last has faded away the clarinet follows suit. However, its newly found freedom from introspective thought is only short-lived. Hardly has it set its ostinato in motion than the harp, which had previously had a somewhat shadowy role, silences it peremptorily.

Endless Parade (71) is scored for trumpet, vibraphone and an orchestra of twenty-four strings grouped in a variety of ways. It owes a great deal to *Melencolia 1* but only in a negative way. Birtwistle deliberately reversed what the earlier work set out to do. There is no exchange of roles, and instead of having a melancholic as protagonist it has an instrument whose nature is outward-looking and ebullient. The title comes from a visit he paid to the Italian town of Lucca, 'a medieval labyrinth of streets encircled by impressive walls'. One of its churches even has a labyrinth carved on its façade.

'My visit coincided with Festa, and a long procession of *tableaux vivants* snaked its way through the narrow streets. I became interested in the number of ways you could observe this event: as a bystander, watching each float pass by, each strikingly individual yet part of a whole; or you could wander through the side alleys, hearing the parade a street away, glimpsing it at a corner, meeting head-on what a moment before you saw from behind. Each time the viewpoint was different, yet instantly identified as part of one body.'

This provides a graphic description of the way Birtwistle's musical 'objects' are introduced, varied, rearranged, expanded or reduced to fragments. Whenever a 'viewpoint' changes, he marks it with a thick bar line in the score. Sometimes the changes occur after a second or two, so following the work with a score helps to identify the different perspectives adopted in the kaleidoscopic state of affairs. His main concern, however, is with the relationship of trumpet and strings and for this no score is needed.

He divides the work into four main sections. The first introduces the principal events, the second 'develops' them in a series of fast episodes, the third in a series of slow ones, while the last returns to the tempo of the first and functions as a coda.

His sketches for the work are some of the most detailed he has made in recent years. As always he starts with a symmetric formulation which on this occasion is implied rather than stated.

The sketches begin with these notes arranged into five seven-note scales all starting on F♯ and ending on the F a diminished octave above. The second of them (F♯–G♯–A–C♯–D–E–F) is used

for the all-important opening trumpet gesture. At first he merely
rhythmizes the notes.

After several recastings of this, he finally comes up with the
version in the score.

We have to wait until the coda before we hear this again in full.
But throughout the work Birtwistle uses the first four notes of
this final version (B–A♯–G–F♯) to remind us of it. When it does
recur in full, it sounds very like the recapitulation of the first
subject in a sonata form. Birtwistle refuses to accept this; nevertheless it does give the impression that a goal had been achieved,
and it does return to the opening 'key'. The fact that the work
starts with the strings and vibraphone playing D and F♯ as a
major third suggests that he has chosen to begin in the traditional trumpet key of D major. D is certainly prominent throughout the piece, but it is always in conflict with symmetric formations pivoting around B or a notional note midway between B
and C. It is only in the coda where the opening gesture is stated
twice that D becomes a much stronger pole of attraction. Even so
D major is not confirmed until the very last chord. The title of

the work is therefore a misnomer. Although the parade may have seemed unending in the streets of Lucca, no other piece of his terminates so conclusively, not even *Earth Dances*.

Initially the trumpet's role was to be that of the golden boy. But since it had to be a virtuoso work making use of a range of material and technical problems, including the playing of fundamental notes which sound very much like the blowing of raspberries, the role changed into that of a boy who is high-spirited, humorous and infinitely curious, but who has absolutely no ambitions to be a goody-goody. This meant that the strings had to be his sidekicks. As well as being collaborators they would also have to act as foils to his ebullience. On the first page of his sketches Birtwistle says that the relationship between them should be that of a 'simultaneous contrast: sun and moon'.

In these circumstances it would be impossible for the trumpet and strings to exchange roles. Certainly the strings would never be able to emulate the character the trumpet has to assume. On the other hand it is perfectly possible for the trumpet to pick up and exploit material introduced by the strings. Being essentially a *continuum* group, most of this consists of varied ostinatos. As these enable the trumpet to show off aspects of its technique such as tonguing to their best advantage, there are long periods when the *cantus* has to give way to them. During these periods the relationship between trumpet and strings is at its closest. Nevertheless, by means of the four-note abbreviated form of its opening gesture, the trumpet concludes each of these episodes by affirming its authoritative role as soloist. Eventually, in the coda, it goes one step further. Here the full version of its opening gesture occurs twice. The trigger for the second appearance is a passage in which the trumpet and strings together contribute to the production of a single line by hocketing. The word 'hoquet' in French means hiccup, and in medieval music the term was used for those passages in which a rhythm is divided between two or more voices each taking one note at a time so that the individual parts sounded just like a series of hiccups. In this case the hockets in the trumpet and those in the strings interlock to create a composite line. Perhaps no technique other than playing in unison can imply so vividly that the participants are at one with each other. Yet the piece has got to end with the trumpet asserting its dominance. The relationship must return to that of sun and moon. Hence the need to restate the gesture which established the brilliance of its character.

HOQUETUS DAVID

Endless Parade received its first performance in Zürich in May 1987. Birtwistle had hoped that the British première might be given at the 1987 Summerscope Festival on the South Bank, which he had been asked to devise, but as the first performance in this country had been promised to the BBC for its January 1988 Festival of Birtwistle's music in the Barbican Centre, the idea had to be abandoned. The section of Summerscope he was responsible for involved twenty-two concerts over a period of thirteen days, and took its title from Giles Farnabye's collection of virginal pieces, *His Fancie, His Toye, His Dreame*, suitably changed into 'Harrison Birtwistle: his fancies, his toys, his dreams'. 'If you ask a composer to plan a series of concerts,' he wrote in his introduction to them, 'you expect the music to carry forward some of his own creative occupations, and also to have a more eccentric view of music than in usual in programme planning.'

One of the first ideas he put to the composer and critic, Bayan Northcott, who assisted him in the planning, consisted of the Masses by Machaut and Stravinsky separated by solo cello pieces by Xenakis. This juxtaposition of the old and the new which had been a creative feature of London's concert life in the fifties and sixties, in contrast to the compartmentalizing of programmes in more recent years, was the principle Birtwistle adopted for all the concerts. Apart from keyboard fantasias by Mozart, Beethoven, Brahms and Liszt, which represented 'a history of music without the sonata', he included nothing from the eighteenth and nine-teenth centuries. 'I want to do lots of polyphony,' he told Northcott, 'nobody does polyphony these days – only it should be Pérotin with saxophones.'

This last remark refers to his opposition to the vogue for period instruments and 'authenticity' in the performance of old music – 'Only through bringing something of the present century to it can we bring this music alive.' It was for this reason as well as the desire to give the series a focus that he asked ten composers to join him in making arrangements of Machaut's *Hoquetus David* to start each programme, his only condition being that the arrangement should be for those musicians taking part in the concert. This meant that Dominic Muldowney, for example, had to make a version for Peter Donohoe, Anthony Gilbert for the Arditti String Quartet, and Birtwistle himself for the English Northern Philharmonia.

Altogether he has made five arrangements of *Hoquetus David*. The first, a fairly straightforward version for two clarinets and bassoon, dates from when he was a student at the Royal Manchester College of Music. In 1969 he scored the much more elaborate second version for the six members of the Pierrot Players. Then came this orchestral version in 1987. The follow-ing year he revised it and made it the centrepiece of a work for the Hamburg Philharmonic Orchestra, and in 1995 he wrote one for two flutes and piccolo trumpet to celebrate Pierre Boulez's seventieth birthday. Over the years the versions have become more elaborate and more personal. Indeed the last completely overrides the letter of Machaut's piece and preserves only its spirit. Likewise Birtwistle's arrangements of chorale preludes by Bach have become freer over the years as can be seen if his 1975 arrangements of five of them are compared with the eight he arranged in 1996 for *Bach Measures* (102).

Birtwistle says the strange rhythmical articulation of *Hoquetus David* and its process of perpetual discontinuity make it sound arcane. Scholars describe it as a textless isorhythmic motet for three voices which Machaut calls tenor, hoquetus and triplum. All make use of hocketing, but only the tenor is isorhythmic, the other two voices are free. In the first part of the work, eight cycles of an eleven-bar *talea* are contained within three cycles of a 32-note *color*; in the second, four cycles of a new nine-bar *talea* are contained within one cycle of the same *color*. The work was composed sometime between 1349 and 1363, but in many respects it is closer to motets composed a century earlier than to those of its own time. Its old-fashioned *modus* notation, 9/8 rhythm, pungent harmony and frequent use of parallel fifths would have made it sound strange and arresting even to Machaut's contemporaries.

Although textless, the work is laid out for three tenors covering a range from the D below middle C to the B above it. The parts frequently cross and the texture they make rarely goes beyond an octave at any one time. This means that arrangements for more than three instruments have to find convincing ways to expand the range and fill out the texture. Birtwistle's 1969 arrangement for the Pierrot Players (30) is scored for flute doubling piccolo, clarinet in C, violin, cello, glockenspiel and tubular bells. His intention was to make it sound as if it were being played on an early medieval organ of the kind that when a note is struck you hear the fifth and octave above it as well. With such an instrument the player could produce three-part organum by simply depressing one key at a time. At first Birtwistle has only two of the three voices doubled in strict organum, but when he gets to the second part, where the bells peal out the tenor line, all three voices are doubled and mordents are added to the principal notes. No period instrument could ever have produced anything as exuberant and fantastic.

He entitled his arrangement for the Summerscope Festival *Les Hoquets du Gardien de la Lune* (73), not just because as a resident of Lunegarde he felt justified in calling himself a guardian of the moon, but because it is much closer to his own music than the previous one. Indeed, apart from being in the mixolydian mode and having a metre that never changes, it could be an original piece. In his programme note he described it as 'an arrangement of my second arrangement, a sort of second stage Chinese Whisper, this time with a pulse of 156'. In fact the arrangement sounds completely different from the version made for the Pierrot Players so that the Chinese Whisper must have gone beyond its second stage. Instead of having to provide parts for six players, he had to write for eight woodwind, ten brass, two percussionists and a five-part string section. This meant that he had to find other ways of thickening the texture. At the opening of the work, for example, the tenor line is distributed across six octaves. Those providing it are double basses, third trumpet, piccolo and second violins playing artificial harmonics. The triplum and hoquetus, on the other hand, are distributed across two and a half octaves. Two trumpets play the lines more or less 'straight' in the middle of the range, while first violins an octave above them and violas an octave below them play rearranged versions of their notes in a different rhythm and with newly composed links between the phrases. To add zest to the texture, the percussion and cellos playing pizzicato create a cross-rhythm by emphasizing some of the off-beat articulations in the composite patterns of durations. Shortly afterwards the lines pass to different instruments, and other forms of doubling and elaborating appear so that the texture never ceases to change.

In 1988, when he composed *Machaut à ma manière* (76) for the Hamburg Philharmonic Orchestra, Birtwistle revised the orchestration and layout of *Les Hoquets du Gardien de la Lune*, added a short interlude at figure 29 of the new score, and completely rewrote the passage between figures 30 and 36. The complete work opens with an arrangement of the isorhythmic motet *Fons totius – O livoris*, and ends with a brief and much altered version of the Amen to the Gloria in *La Messe de Nostre-Dame*. The *talea* and *color* in *Fons totius –O livoris* are out of step with each other at the beginning. But the feature that interested Birtwistle was that short isorhythmic sections keep recurring in the triplum and motetus so that he was able to make his arrangement sound as if it were constructed in the form of verse and refrain.

Hoquetus Petrus (94), the extremely free arrangement he made to celebrate Boulez's seventieth birthday, is a *bonne bouche* lasting only a few minutes. The similarities to Machaut's work are merely its scoring for three instruments, its triple-time metre and its hocketing. The instruments are two flutes (the first doubling piccolo) and a piccolo trumpet, and Birtwistle has them playing at the top of their registers on several occasions. This means that the tessitura lies some two octaves above the Machaut. He constructed the piece from a series of varied ostinatos moving within a fixed harmonic framework, an octave E. To all intents and purposes, the three instruments sound like a dawn chorus. Birdsong appears at the end of *Gawain* when Morgan goes outside, and in *The Second Mrs Kong* (90) when Kong and the Head of Orpheus come out of the world of shadows and enter the world of the living. In these instances the instruments are meant to represent real birds, but in *Carmen Arcadiae Mechanicae Perpetuum* (53), which, as mentioned earlier, takes its title from Paul Klee's *Twittering Machine*, the birds are usually mechanical rather than real. This is why *Hoquetus Petrus* comes to an end sounding as if the mechanisms were winding down.

FOUR SONGS OF AUTUMN – FRIEZE I

The distinguishing features of the relationship between *cantus* and *continuum* in *Secret Theatre* are that they balance each other and run concurrently. In *Earth Dances*, where the *cantus* dominates the first part and the *continuum* the second, this close relationship begins to break down. *Endless Parade* takes the tendency still further. As in *Words Overheard*, the soloist gets drawn into the material of the *continuum* so that during fairly lengthy periods of the work the *cantus* is abandoned. The inevitable consequence of this separation of 'horizontal music'

and 'vertical music' was the emergence of works based exclusively either on 'melodic development' or 'rhythmic development'. Although Birtwistle says that *Hoquetus David* makes its
appeal through its rhythmical articulation and its process of
perpetual discontinuity, the impetus behind it was melodic
rather than rhythmic, i.e., the expansion of a particularly lyrical
section of plainsong. *Hoquetus Petrus*, on the other hand, focuses
on the way 'vertical music' can be developed. And it is not a one-
off. Basing a work on rhythmically orientated patterns operating
within a fixed harmonic framework has become a feature of
several works in recent years. The one that prepared the ground
for them was a cycle of songs Birtwistle called *Four Songs of
Autumn* (74).

They were written to celebrate the twentieth anniversary of
the London Sinfonietta. The Sinfonietta had been championing
his music ever since they commissioned *Verses for Ensembles* in
1968. For its tenth anniversary concert in January 1978, he had
composed *Carmen Arcadiae Mechanicae Perpetuum*, and for this
1988 anniversary he wanted to present it with something equally
startling and unusual. Following on from what he had been
doing to Machaut's motet, he decided to arrange for chamber
choir and an instrumental ensemble *Deowa* (62), his melodically
orientated piece for soprano and clarinet based on the phonemes
contained in its title. He began the task in November 1987, but
it proved to be much more formidable than he anticipated. After
three weeks' work he had only written three pages of sketches
and two pages of a draft. 'I realized,' he said in his programme
note for the *Four Songs of Autumn*, 'that I would not be within
light years of being able to complete it and the project had to be
abandoned. So in a fit of melancholy I wrote these four songs for
soprano and string quartet.'

One of the most striking things about them is that Birtwistle
rarely asks the soprano to sing legato. Her line is continually
broken up so that the emphasis is placed on rhythm. This example comes from the opening of the second song.

♪ = ca.54
p

Beat - ing   their wings a - gainst   the white   clouds,

The songs are settings of four short poems Birtwistle found on
pages 80, 81 and 85 of *The Penguin Book of Japanese Verse*.* The
first, 'The grasses and trees' is by the mid-tenth-century poet
Bunya Yasuhide, while the others, 'Beating their wings', 'When
the moonlight' and 'In the spring haze' come from a group of
anonymous early tenth-century poems contained in *Kokinshu*,
the first Imperial anthology. Bunya Yasuhide's poem gives hint of
a melancholy that has a deeper source than the approach of
winter: 'The grasses and trees / Change their colours; / But to the
wave-blooms / On the broad sea-plain / There comes no autumn.'
The other poems are vignettes dealing with the flight of wild
geese on a moonlit autumn night; the sight of moonlight through
the branches of the bare trees; and the calls of the wild geese
disappearing above the autumn mist.

Just as autumn runs through all the poems, so the pitch class
E runs through all the songs. Throughout the first song the cello
sustains its lowest E as a drone or pedal point. Thereafter the
note works its way up the quartet an octave at a time until it
reaches the open string of the first violin where it has its neighbour notes, D♯ and F, oscillating around it. To draw attention to
the change of octave and the continuing presence of E, Birtwistle
uses the ubiquitous D–F dyad as a marker.

The presence of a single pitch class as a constant point of reference throughout a score is unique in Birtwistle's oeuvre. The
clues to why he decided to make use of it here lie in the poetry,
which exemplifies the principle 'the same but always different',

---

* *The Penguin Book of Japanese Verse*, translated by Geoffrey Bownas and
Anthony Thwaite, Harmondsworth, 1964.

for each poem looks at autumn from a different perspective. The continuing presence of E, the scoring and the sound of muted strings constantly playing on their fingerboards to produce a veiled effect provide the sameness; while the changing harmony and the variety of ostinatos, melodic shapes and distinctive intervals used to characterize each song provide at least some of the differences.

In tonal music the tonic and dominant are thought to be the most suitable notes for pedal points. They frequently lie in the bass, yet there are numerous examples where they appear in an upper or middle voice. As has already been indicated, Birtwistle's E starts in the bass, moves up to two middle voices and finds its destination as an inverted pedal on the first violin. All his harmony is built around a framework of fifths. In the first song these are E–B–F♯–C♯–G♯. The cello plays the pedal point, the viola and second violin take the B, the first violin has the F♯ and the soprano the C♯ and G♯. By involving the adjacencies to their notes, the strings supply a background *continuum* of ostinatos and sustain a basically unchanging harmony. The soprano, on the other hand, creates a sense of forward movement through the scale-based line she is given, even though for the sake of the rhythmic articulation it is fractured. Her notes have their origin in a seven-note chromatic scale with its axis of symmetry on B. To obtain the necessary fifth between C♯ and G♯, its last two notes (A and G♯) have to be transposed up an octave.

The essential idea behind Bunya Yasuhide's poem is that there are places beyond the terrestrial where nothing changes colour and there is 'no autumn'. Birtwistle highlights the importance of these words by withholding a stress on C♯ and the appearance of A♯ until they occur.

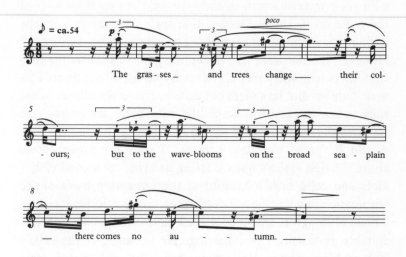

Here the distinctive interval is a fifth. In the next song it will be a sixth and in the following one a seventh. The second and third songs are based on the same principles as the first but varied to suit the poetry. In the second the fifths are A–E–B–F♯–C♯ while the soprano's underlying scale has its axis of symmetry on C♯; in the third they are D–A–E–B–F♯ and the scale has its axis of symmetry on E. In both songs the accompanying instruments extend their range by drawing on the adjacencies surrounding the basic notes of their colleagues as well as their own for their ostinatos. This applies particularly to the third song where the poetic image is of moonlight seen through the bare branches of the trees. To produce the necessary diaphanous texture, Birtwistle places rests between all the notes in the accompaniment other than the pedal point (as indeed he had also done in the previous song), and scatters the fifths across a much wider spectrum than hitherto.

In that it involves harmonic and textual changes, the fourth song needs a different structure from the first three. The text deals with two moods rather than a single one. On the basis that

wild geese migrate north in early spring, the first three lines of
the poem create the impression that spring has arrived: 'In the
spring haze / Dim, disappearing, / The wild geese are calling . . .'
However, the last line, 'Above autumn's mist', shatters the illusion. Birtwistle still bases his harmony on fifths, but he reduces
their number and lays them out differently. At the climax of the
song, when the soprano sings 'the wild geese are calling', he
captures the excitement of spring by framing the passage with
A and E spread over two octaves. Within the upper octave
above the first violin's open E string he gives the second violin,
viola and cello each a handful of the remaining notes of the
chromatic scale and out of them they create a leaping texture
which, although it has to be played pianissimo, is nevertheless
suitably ebullient. The following, for instance, is the cello's
line, which draws its notes from the chromatic scale
G♯–A–B♭–B–C–C♯–D–D♯–E.

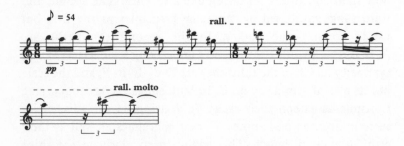

Although this is based on the adjacencies surrounding A and
E, it is actually compounded from two lines both gravitating in
terms of their voice-leading (part-writing) towards C♯.

When thoughts of spring have to be abandoned, the music drops to its lowest register, all the instruments except the first violin play in rhythmic unison with the soprano, and the harmony loses its airiness to become opaque. A and E are still present but their adjacencies have been transposed to lower regions. Yet, as well as taking the adjacencies to the perfect intervals of fourth, fifth and octave into account when analysing Birtwistle's harmony, the importance of voice-leading must be stressed again.

An 'abstract' of the harmony in the last few bars.

However, the wild geese have not been completely lost sight of. When the harmony has reached its darkest, the first violin brings the work to a close by taking the music high 'above autumn's mist'. Throughout the whole of the song, it has been playing in its own time an ostinato involving D♯ and F, the closest adjacencies to E, but in its final passage it changes D♯ into E♭ and incorporates G. As well as balancing the notes C♯–D♯–E which the cello played before the beginning of the first song in the cycle (C♯–D♯–E/E–F–G), the inclusion of G may also suggest that although the birds are flying off, their departure can be viewed as the advent of something new.

Previously Birtwistle had only consistently used fifths as a harmonic framework in *Monody for Corpus Christi* (2), his three-movement 'cantata' for soprano, flute, violin and horn. Their use had been put into his mind when he read about Gustav Holst going into Thaxted Parish Church during the First World War and seeing a woman wandering up and down the aisles singing to the accompaniment of the open strings of her violin. Although the notes of the open strings occur only intermittently in Birtwistle's work, they nevertheless provide his highly diversified monody with fixed points of reference.

In 1991 when he was asked to compose a piece for string quartet to celebrate the ninetieth birthday of Alfred Schlee of Universal Edition in Vienna, he produced another piece based on open strings: this time those of the cello and viola as well as the violin. It is in this piece that 'vertical music' – music based exclusively on rhythmical as opposed to melodic development – comes into its own. Birtwistle makes his intentions clear on his first page of sketches. Normally he would have started with a symmetric pitch formulation, but in this instance he begins with a rhythmic pattern divided into six units.

This takes pride of place in the left-hand corner of the large sheet of manuscript paper. Next to it is a chart consisting of three staves containing seventeen bars. The staves represent the two violins and the viola, the bars the sections into which the work as a whole is going to be divided. In each bar one of the staves has been blocked out with a black pencil so that visually the chart looks like the pattern one might see on a frieze. This must have occurred to Birtwistle too, but instead of writing 'frieze' beneath it he wrote 'freeze'. At first sight this appears to be a misspelling, yet the word 'freeze' occurs over and over again in his scores. It nearly always means that the performers should stop playing or singing and remain absolutely still. But he also uses the word 'frozen' when he refers to music that may be vigorous on the surface but is harmonically frozen within its own narrow orbit as is the case with many of his ostinatos. So that although he eventually chose 'frieze' for the title of his piece, its homophone could well have been a viable alternative.

In the centre of this first page of sketches are the notes around which his ostinatos will oscillate.

Beneath this and dominating the whole of the bottom half of the first page is another chart. This one is devoted to permutations of the rhythm's six units arranged into 200 groups of three. Although these may result in music that oscillates within narrow bounds and fails to develop, the piece as a whole turned out to be extremely dynamic, the reason being that there are two other rhythmic strata pitted against these ostinatos, and both are developmental. One is based on a triplet figuration and appears mostly in the cello, the other is given mainly to the first violin and at times could almost be deemed a *cantus*. As well as being built from the adjacencies surrounding fifths and octaves, it also makes use of scalic figurations, and as in *Four Songs of Autumn* it is these that provide the piece with the necessary degree of linear direction.

SALFORD TOCCATA

The problem of how to keep music moving forward, especially in an opera where many of the events involve cyclic return, concerned Birtwistle deeply during the year when he was waiting to get started on *Gawain*. This is one of the reasons why he embarked on an intensive study of *The Ring* during 1988, and why he welcomed the opportunity to write a piece for the brass band of Salford College of Technology. Among other things he was able to develop new ways of creating tension and momentum.

Salford Toccata is the second work he has written for brass band. He knew it would have to be a toccata even when he was composing his previous piece, *Grimethorpe Aria* (45), in 1974. I think this was because he equated the sound of a brass band with that of an organ, and his ambition was to write a triptych that would be to the brass band what Bach's Toccata, Adagio and Fugue (BWV 564) is to the organ. He would still like to complete the work by writing a fugue, but the brass band world has changed since the days when Elgar Howarth conducted the Grimethorpe Colliery Band. Nowadays bands spend most of their time learning the test pieces for the various competitions they go in for and are not prepared to learn difficult and really worthwhile works. What time they have at their disposal is devoted to ear-tickling fare. 'In any case,' says Birtwistle, 'who would want to play or listen to a triptych for brass lasting for nearly forty-five minutes?'

Like *An Imaginary Landscape*, *Grimethorpe Aria* is a piece for choirs of brass instruments that reaches its conclusion when the lyrical material it has been nurturing is finally allowed to blossom into an elegiac cantilena. *Salford Toccata*, on the other hand, is based mainly on layers of Birtwistle's highly idiosyncratic varied ostinatos. In this respect it is not unlike *Earth Dances*. Where it differs from the orchestral work is that instead of relying on climactic build-ups to create momentum it draws on textural and formal procedures.

Although Monteverdi called the fanfare that opens *Orfeo* a toccata, the term is usually used for keyboard pieces intended to show off the dextrous 'touch' of the performer. Since the eighteenth century most toccatas have been in the form of a *perpetuum mobile* based on running semiquavers. As far as *Salford Toccata* is concerned, Birtwistle takes this as being the toccata style, but instead of establishing the constant semiquaver movement immediately, as Debussy does in the toccata in *Pour le piano*, for example, he leads up to it gradually. The four sections into which the work is divided all begin and develop in different ways but they culminate in semiquavers. However, these semiquavers are never presented by the whole band or sections of the band playing in rhythmic unison – they are always the outcome of several independent rhythmic patterns superimposed on each other. As in *Grimethorpe Aria*, the band is divided into choirs or layers that can vary in their membership. At the culmination of the first section, for instance, there are five. The first contains nine cornets, the second three E♭ horns and two baritones, the third three trombones and two euphoniums, the fourth two E♭ bass tubas, and the fifth two BB♭ bass tubas. Although coordinated by a regular 3/8 metre, each choir has its own rhythm and consequently its own character. They produce the regular semiquaver movement through a form of hocketing.

The music leading up to these culminating passages uses these layers in two other distinctive ways. The first is to intertwine them so that they constantly overlap each other. When one is drawing to a conclusion another is starting out or establishing itself. The texture is therefore in a constant state of flux. This is the technique which Birtwistle employs to even greater effect in *Gawain*. The other is the dramatic conflict between music based on 'rhythmic development' and that based on 'melodic development'. Throughout the second and third sections in particular melodic material is constantly trying to establish itself in one way or another, but at every stage it has to give way to the much more assertive rhythmic element in the music. It is this conflict which produces the tension and creates the momentum. In this piece, unlike so many of his other substantial works in a single span, Birtwistle has no need to generate energy towards a climax. Climaxes are replaced by the passages in which constant semi-quavers are produced. Nevertheless there is one moment just after the third section has run its course that could be considered climactic even though the music lies in a low register. It immediately follows the long descending scale Birtwistle has been using to terminate the sections. In this instance, however, instead of taking the music to where it can begin again, this particular 'ladder' leads to the alternation of the notes A and E♭ played low down by the four bass tubas. The sound could be his justification for choosing a line from William Blake to preface the score: 'Here mountains of brass promise much riches in their dreadful bosoms'. But those who are familiar with *The Ring* may recognize its similarity to the music Wagner used for the death of Fafner in the second act of *Siegfried*. There a bass tuba and a contrabass tuba also alternate between A and E♭ in the same very low register. Had Birtwistle included Wagner's timpani and double basses, which between them articulate the rhythm associated with the giants, the reference would have been too obvious for the context.

Originally it was the music of *Götterdämmerung* which attracted him to *The Ring*, but with *Gawain* in mind it was inevitable that *Siegfried* should take priority. After all, it too concerns a golden boy who goes on a journey that results in self-knowledge. However, apart from this fleeting reference to the death of Fafner, *Salford Toccata* reflects very little of the influence of Wagner. Indeed Birtwistle's handling of the one and only motif in the work is closer to Schubert than to Wagner. Like Schubert in the first movement of the Piano Sonata in C minor (D.958), for instance, he takes a single interval as a point of reference, but every time it occurs he changes its character. Schubert chose a falling semitone for this particular movement, giving special emphasis to the semitone between A♭ and G. He may keep on returning to these notes yet they never sound the same because their harmonization differs. Birtwistle, on the other hand, once more opted for a rising minor third. In *Secret Theatre, Earth Dances* and *Four Songs of Autumn*, where it was the fixed D/F motif, it tended to retain the initial character given to it. But here, where it is transposed to a variety of pitches, its character undergoes a series of transformations. It first appears near the beginning of the work as E/G and sounds like a distant call, something beckoning us. But when the same notes recur near the end of the work they poignantly herald a passage in which it would seem that the melodic material with which the rising minor third has been associated throughout the work has at last come into its own. Birtwistle uses the flugelhorn to draw out the interval as if the music were about to blossom into something lyrical and life enhancing. But in the event it gives way to percussive semiquavers produced by hocketing cornets, horns and first baritone. Underneath them there is an equally drawn-out minor third between C and E♭ played on trombones, euphoniums and tubas. In this context and orchestration it sounds ominous. Justifiably so, for the work ends abruptly with a mighty crash from a very large bass drum, an instrument Birtwistle has reserved specially for this occasion in this score. To help them to sustain its reverberations, he asks the two BB♭ basses to play their lowest possible pedal. The end of the piece is therefore as violent and bloodcurdling as Fafner's.

WORKS FOCUSING ON MELODY

In April 1988, some six months before he embarked on *Salford Toccata*, Birtwistle wrote a song containing a melodic line the singer cannot sustain throughout its duration because the text becomes too broken up for lyricism. It has to be continued by instruments. The song was composed for the eightieth birthday of Sir William Glock who had brought his distinguished career to a conclusion by becoming the BBC's Controller of Music. It was he who inaugurated the Tuesday Invitation Concerts in

which the old and the new were juxtaposed in a highly imaginative way, and which no serious musician of Birtwistle's generation could afford to ignore. For his text Birtwistle chose to set
Rilke's *An die Musik* (75), not only because it is a celebration of
music and therefore pertinent to its dedicatee, but because it
suggests that our experience of music can have the concreteness
of a pure 'thing', an idea which Birtwistle, given his constant
reference to music as a series of objects, is not unsympathetic. To
use the language usually employed when discussing Rilke, it can
be an emotional communion with the non-personal ground of
being. In the process of exploring this idea, the poem becomes
increasingly introspective and hesitant. Gradually lines are
reduced to single words: *da uns das Innre umsteht / als geübteste
Ferne, als andre / Seite der Luft: / rein, / riesig, / nicht mehr bewohnbar*
('where what is within us / as practised horizon, as other / side of
the air: / pure, / gigantic, / no longer lived in;' (translated by
J.B. Leishman).

In his programme note about the song, Birtwistle drew attention to the fact that he too was juxtaposing the old and the new.
'The piece,' he wrote, 'contains references to the *An die Musik* of
Schubert and also a very dim memory of a piece by Bruno
Maderna heard in a Tuesday Invitation Concert many years ago.'
It is scored for soprano and ten instruments, and it falls into four
sections. The first is given over to the highest form of lyricism –
three melismatic settings of the word *Musik*. Then when the text
begins to become explorative each syllable is given a separate
note with only occasional snatches of melisma. In the third
section a tambourine enters in order to throw the listener's attention on to rhythm. Finally rhythm takes over. In a situation
where the soprano's line is split up with rests and the melodic
texture given to oboe, bassoon and first violin gradually drift
away, the only thing that remains constant is a toccata-like flow
of demisemiquavers on the flute and clarinet.

It could be said that after this the situation was ripe for *Salford
Toccata*. Nevertheless, in March 1989, immediately after he had

completed the brass band piece, he wrote a song in which melody is paramount. Scored for soprano, two clarinets, viola, cello and double bass it is a setting of White and Light (78), a translation by Michael Hamburger of a poem by Paul Celan which he found in a poetry magazine. Although an avid reader of poetry, Birtwistle had not come across Paul Celan's work before. 'I was attracted by the imagery,' he says, 'the lyrical quality, its "setability", surrealism and the way it seemed to be groping for words and for meaning.' Since obtaining a copy of Hamburger's translation of most of Celan's poems* in the early nineties he has set eight more, and it is now difficult to imagine that he would ever want to set anyone else's verse. Celan was a Romanian who wrote exclusively in German, the language of those who, during the war, imprisoned his parents in a concentration camp, shot his mother for being unfit for work and sent him to a labour camp. Although Michael Hamburger says that anguish, darkness and the shadow of death are present in all his poems' even the most high-spirited and sensuous,† the reader would have to be familiar with a great many of them to detect these qualities in *White and Light*. An uninitiated reader would have no reason to equate 'sleep' with death in this context. To all intents and purposes it is a love poem in which the images are connected with the seashore. Central to Birtwistle's setting are the words 'drift' and 'mirroring'. Lines 20 to 24, for example, read: 'The drift that beckons from cliffs. / It beckons / brows to come near, / those brows we were lent / for mirroring's sake.'

Although he must have known what the accompaniment would have to be before composing the song – for it is here that the images of drifting and mirroring find musical expression – he nevertheless wrote the vocal line first, and when he talks about the song he gives the impression that this was unusual.

---

* *Poems of Paul Celan*, tr. Michael Hamburger, Anvil Press Poetry, London 1988.

† *Paul Celan, Selected Poems*, tr. Michael Hamburger and Christopher Middleton, Harmondsworth 1972, p.13.

Apparently, he made no sketches for the work and the one and only draft reveals that he wrote the vocal line straight out – neatly and with very few alterations.

At the top of the first page Birtwistle has written: 'The voice part must be mainly quiet and introspective, the instrumental parts a mere shadow of it.' The most obvious form of shadowing takes place in the clarinets. Between them they create a smoother, more sustained version of the singer's line, sometimes anticipating what she is about to sing, at other times echoing her. The effect is like a stream of three-part heterophony. A considerably less obvious form takes place in the cello and double bass. They too produce a line in which the notes overlap each other. But in this case it only vaguely shadows what the singer is doing. On the whole it appears to be a distorted mirror image of her line even though there are phrases that sound more like a deformed echo than a mutilated inversion. The shadow least like the vocal line is the one given to the viola, but it is here that we get the strongest sense of drifting. Throughout the song it has a *perpetuum mobile* meandering around the notes of its middle two open strings, D and G, its motion being suspended only on two short occasions. The first is when the soprano says, 'White / what moves us,/ without weight / what we exchange./ White and Light: / let it drift', the second when she asks, 'Are you asleep?' Although the viola's music may spring from the soprano's, it nevertheless has all the mannerisms of one of Birtwistle's typical varied ostinatos. It functions as a *continuum*.

About a year after writing *White and Light*, Birtwistle interrupted work on *Gawain* to compose *Ritual Fragment* (80), another piece entirely given over to melody. It was written for the London Sinfonietta to play at the memorial concert for Michael Vyner, who had been the ensemble's highly valued artistic director since 1972. The work has to be performed without a conductor, and is scored for the Sinfonietta's usual complement of fourteen players, except that in this case the trombonist has to play a bass trumpet. The only percussion instrument is a large bass drum set horizontally and placed in a prominent position at the front of the playing area. Next to it is a solo position occupied in turn by ten of the players who between them unfold the melody in a manner appropriate to the nature of their instruments. They are those who play trumpet, violin 1, bassoon, viola, horn, oboe, violin 2, clarinet, bass trumpet and flute. After delivering their tributes, the instrumentalists rejoin their colleagues sitting further back and playing the accompaniment.

Birtwistle's sketches for the work are almost exclusively devoted to the melody. Nevertheless they begin with those for the two chords which open the work, the first being a rearrangement of a symmetric scale centred on D. It is from these chords that the trumpet's melody emerges, and when this is established it becomes apparent that Birtwistle's prime concern lies in the way the line develops. A typical example is the way the first violin develops and transforms a phrase of four notes that brings the trumpet's solo to an end. It begins by doubling the trumpet. But in the following three versions its double stopping, ponticello, tremolo and harmonics transform the four notes into music only a violin could play. The same applies to the passages (here omitted) that connect the four versions. These draw on other types of violin technique.

The connections between the first three versions can easily be heard, but the last seems to have been transformed beyond recognition. Its relationship to the others can be explained only in terms of its intervallic content. Arranging intervals into symmet-rically ordered scales and patterns had been a component of Birtwistle's technique for years. But, judging by the sketches, they seem to be particularly important in this work. On page 10, for instance, he writes out a symmetric pattern of intervals which could be the basis of a melody consisting of four five-note phrases: 1221–1122–2112–2211. There are no sketches for the violin's variants of the four-note figure given above, but the intervallic pattern they produce is 242–112–122–242. The fact that the last version inverts the notes of the first and stretches the major third into a major tenth is simply part of the developmen-tal process. Its ascent into the stratosphere, however, suggests that the figure has reached its culmination and has to be super-seded by something else. This becomes evident when the bassoon enters. It develops a gesture in one of the violin's linking passages.

Apart from one for the funeral march rhythm on the bass drum, which opens the work and keeps on returning from time to time regardless of what is happening in the melody, there are no sketches at all for the accompaniment. But this does not mean it lacks interest. Basically it contains three elements: ostinatos based on fragments of the cantus, snatches of music which the erstwhile soloists quote after they have returned to their seats, and a series of what can only be called 'sad songs'. The first of these is given to the flute and occurs when the horn is giving way to the oboe in the solo line. But instead of reflecting on what is happening in the *cantus*, it follows its own course, floating high above the other instruments and appearing to be quite indepen-dent of them, both in musical content and mood.

To a certain extent the relationship between melody and accompaniment in *Ritual Fragment* reflects that in *Gawain*, where the orchestra shadows the vocal line but nevertheless has a life of its own. But when Birtwistle completed the opera he wrote a set of songs for the Aldeburgh Festival in which he took the inde-pendence of melody and accompaniment even further. They are settings for soprano and thirteen instruments of four poems by the Estonian poet, Jaan Kaplinski, which he came across when browsing in a London bookstore. His interest, he said, was triggered by what the poet had written in his introduction:

> To occupy oneself with biology and nature in practice as well as in theory is a vast and noble undertaking. This begins with the observation of nature: photographing birds, feeding animals, describing plants; and ends with a universal science of nature which transforms the world into what I have previously called Utopia, and what formerly was called the realm of peace, The Golden Age.

That Birtwistle felt this applied to himself can be confirmed by what his son Silas, then aged nine, once wrote of him. At the time the family lived in Twickenham, and Silas's father worked in a hut near the bottom of the garden:

> Most people write about my fathers music. I am going to write about some other things to do with him. In his hut (which would make a supper space module) he gave me a few piano lessons, but I had to stop becos he is busy at the moment. He keeps fossils and lots of other things like skulls of animals and birds. He also has an armey of little woden animals which my brother bought him for his Birthday (and which we all go in and arrange when he is not in) outside his window he has made a bird tabal on which he puts crums and bits of fat so that birds will come and he can take photographes of them. When he comes out of his hut, he *always* looks rounds the garden. We have lots of old roses and plants and ferns. He is looking at them now on his way in for lunch.

Although all four of the Kaplinski poems he selected draw on nature for their images, the poet's main preoccupation seems to be with ambiguously placing side by side two widely dissimilar images so that the end result has something mystical about it. No other poem summarizes this so succinctly as the last:

> THE WAY TURNS toward the heath
> dead windmills stand
> against darkness
> in the whole world
> there is nothing
> but the scent of red clover
> and nothing more*

The most striking thing about Birtwistle's work is the way the soaring, intensely expressive vocal line contrasts with the sombre accompaniment. It is as if Birtwistle had found another way of applying the principle of the juxtaposition of opposites. To enhance the contrast there is a short instrumental interlude between each song. All three are based on a rhythmic figure the flute has picked up from the singer in the first song. This means that although melodic development is the focus for the songs, in the interludes rhythmic development takes over. In the last song, however, the two come together, for in this the piano takes up and develops a rhythmic figure in the preceding interlude. But whereas the soprano gets increasingly more ecstatic during its course, the accompaniment becomes increasingly starker.

Some of the sketches for the work are missing, but those that are contained in the Paul Sacher Foundation suggest from the consistent neatness of the vocal line that once again it was composed first and without hesitation. Most of Birtwistle's efforts were devoted to the accompaniment, or rather to the symmetric patterns of intervals from which he could build the

---

* From 'The Same Sea in Us All', Breitbush Books, Portland, Oregon 1985. Reproduced by kind permission of the translator, Sam Hamill, and Cooper Canyon Press, Port Townsend, Washington.

chords that punctuate the work and become particularly prominent when given to the piano in the last song. Strangely enough,
although the scoring is for string quintet, wind quintet, trumpet,
piano and harp, most of these chords are based on the open
strings of the violin. At one stage, for instance, he writes two
lines of four-note groups all with the open D as the lowest note.
The intervals between the notes in the first line are: 427 –
526–625–724; while beneath this in the second line he continues
this palindromic patterning with 518–617–716–815. Adjacent to
these are charts indicating ways in which these can be combined
or permutated. In themselves they may not be particularly interesting, but they stand in vivid contrast to the spontaneity of the
vocal line, and it is this relationship which gives the work its
special identity. Significantly, within six months Birtwistle was
to compose *An Interrupted Endless Melody* (85) where, as discussed
in the first part of this chapter, melody and accompaniment are
totally dissociated.

GAWAIN'S MUSIC

Birtwistle refuses to have a gramophone, cassette or CD player in
his house so that when he wanted to hear *The Ring* he had to get
his wife to drive him slowly along the country roads of Lot while
he listened to it on cassette in the car with the score propped up
on his lap. The first live performance he heard was at Bayreuth
in 1992. *Siegfried* was of particular interest not just because it too
was about a golden boy, but because, as the comic opera in
Wagner's trilogy, it contains many more formal set pieces than
Die Walküre or *Götterdämmerung*. And it does so without any
sacrifice of the sense of organic development which is one of the
most characteristic features of *The Ring*. The first scene in Act
One between Mime and Siegfried, for instance, is built around
five songs each of which could have been self-contained had
Wagner provided them with a firm tonic cadence when they
come to an end. Instead he takes them straight into a transition

section where he prepares the ground for the next song. It becomes evident that his purpose in providing Mime and Siegfried with songs is that he wants to focus on certain aspects of their characters rather the dramatic situation they are involved in. The background to who and what they are comes mainly from the orchestra, whose function in *The Ring* is not unlike that of the unseen, yet all-knowing narrator in a nineteenth-century novel. In Wagner's hands the orchestra not only accompanies and sets the scene, it can also, through the use of motifs, draw parallels, relate present to past, anticipate the future and enter into the minds of those on stage.

Birtwistle also divides *Gawain* into set pieces and gives great weight to the orchestra, but he makes much less use of transitions and the role of narrator is taken by Morgan so that the orchestra has a different function. It too provides richness and depth; at the same time it manages to suggest the existence of a world lying behind the events on stage and what the characters are singing about. Although its music stems mainly from the vocal line, like so many of Birtwistle's accompaniments during this period it has a life of its own.

Set pieces are actually built into Harsent's libretto, yet in some instances Birtwistle has to change them to make them suitable for the kind of music he wants to write. The six stanzas given to Morgan and Lady de Hautdesert to sing in the opening scene, for instance, have a verbal rhythm that could easily be turned into a strophic song. But this would be alien to Birtwistle's music. So instead each stanza is freely composed and the regularity is confined to a short instrumental refrain. After the last stanza, however, the refrain is replaced by introductory music for the first of Arthur's behests for someone to prove his courage. This is when the action begins, because it is in this episode that we see on a screen a knight travelling through a landscape and hear what Morgan and Lady de Hautdesert have to say about the implications of this for Gawain: 'Soon you'll see its face,/ soon you'll hear its voice.' Yet even though Arthur's calls differ in length (the first is four, the second six, the third eighteen and the fourth eight lines long) Birtwistle still seeks to impose on them the organizing principle of verse/refrain form. This means placing Arthur's refrain 'Who's brave?' at the end rather than at the beginning of the verses as Harsent does. It also means adding another 'Who's brave?' to the text.

He writes for the standard symphony orchestra, but adds a cimbalom and strengthens the bass by including a contrabass clarinet and three tubas, the first doubling euphonium. As well as accompanying the vocal line and giving it depth, the orchestra also has the task of defining the structure of the work. At every formal juncture the orchestration and texture change. As in *Earth Dances* and *Salford Toccata*, Birtwistle divides his forces into layers several lines deep. Frequently there may be three or four of these layers accompanying the voice, but even though quite different from each other all will be 'shadowing' it in ways reminiscent of the shadowing in *White and Light*. In addition to these layers there might also be a line that cuts across the formal divisions. The first to impinge on the ear begins in the fourth stanza of the duet between Morgan and Lady de Hautdesert cited above. It occurs when Lady de Hautdesert talks about the singing and dancing that take place at Christmas. Although suspended during the short refrains, the line continues right up to the end of Arthur's second call. The reason it impinges on the ear is because like the cantus in *Earth Dances* it contains narrow intervals, lies in the middle register and can be easily followed. The practical reason for its presence is to link what Lady de Hautdesert has been saying with Arthur's opening words: ' ... they tire me – rituals of the season tamed by habit'. However, the somewhat sad character of the line is totally at odds with the words and the music Birtwistle gives the singers. In it we get the first glimpse of a world lying behind the action.

In her article 'Gawain's Musical Journey', which appeared in the programme booklet issued by The Royal Opera in 1991,

Rhian Samuel said: '*Gawain* is built on a fundamental melodic line whose progress the composer describes visually in three dimensions – it spirals round a basically circular path (the repeated sections become framed rectangles along the circle).' This suggests that Birtwistle was following a 'pre-compositional' plan, but it is something he hotly denies. There is a fundamental melodic line, he says, but it arose step by step from out of the context. My perusal of the 669 pages of sketches in the Paul Sacher Foundation led me to believe that the line lies mainly in the vocal parts, but as often as not there are also complementary lines lying in the orchestra as well. The vocal line appears to spring from the speech inflections inherent in Harsent's text, the need to make the words as clear as possible and the necessity to reflect the emotional state of the character singing them. As in most of his works composed since the mid-seventies the line arises from the rearrangement of scales containing distinctive patterns of intervals nearly always of a symmetric nature. Birtwistle indicates this in the short orchestral prelude which opens the opera, for here he gives us scales before they have been turned into melodies. Although some are presented as chords, most of them are arranged to form an undulating contour that culminates in a section where falling scales with comparatively narrow intervals are laid against falling scales with comparatively wide ones. As a result we get a foretaste of one of the ways in which Birtwistle will shadow the melodic line when it appears.

With the exception of this prelude, all the music given to the orchestra when not accompanying the vocal line is of the rhythmical as opposed to the melodic type. But none of it is very long because the vocal line is suspended only for relatively short periods. The most extended piece of purely orchestral music occurs when Gawain undertakes the journey north. Yet this is interspersed with vocal passages which break up the orchestra's continuum-like textures. Some of these are devoted to Morgan telling Gawain how far he has to go; others to Bertilak and his wife urging him on, their voices sounding as if they were already welcoming him.

In the seduction scene, the biggest set piece of all, the position is reversed. Here Morgan's lullabies and Lady de Hautdesert's love music dominate the proceedings. The orchestra's role is to insert rhythmic music suitable for the hunting and slaughter of the stag, boar and fox. The killing of the fox takes place just after Gawain has accepted the sash, and together these two events constitute the climax of the scene. But whereas the occasion is one of triumph for Morgan, Lady de Hautdesert now knows that her efforts to seduce Gawain have failed and her love for him is doomed so that for her the occasion is one of anguish. To distinguish between their reactions, Birtwistle has them sing one after the other different versions of the cry 'AEIYA' which he first had them utter during the fifth and climactic section of the masque that ended Act One.* On that occasion he asks them to sing it as if it were 'a war cry', and indeed whenever Morgan delivers it on subsequent occasions it retains this identity. It measures her increasing sense of exultation, and with it she makes her final exit at the very end of the opera. It is also the cry that Lady de Hautdesert utters when she leaves the stage for good except that in her case it measures her despair.

Although none comes back more frequently than 'AEIYA', most of the phrases that mark significant events in the course of the work return at least once. D–F–D♭–E, the four notes used for the moment when the axe strikes its target, appear in Act One when the Green Knight is the victim and in Act Two when Gawain's neck is nicked. Nevertheless only one phrase functions like a Wagnerian leitmotif and that is a short gesture for the three tubas which occurs in the initial court scene after each of the Fool's first three riddles have been answered.

* The cry was invented by Birtwistle. It is not in Harsent's text.

The tubas at fig. 23 in the first act.*

In those incidents, the gesture functions as a refrain rather than a motif. It becomes a motif when Birtwistle brings it back it after the door has mysteriously opened and closed, and Arthur goes on to say, 'It's nothing, a game, an escapade, Christmas mummers, a raree show.' Later, when the door closes after the Green Knight has made his exit, it comes back again. But on this occasion the effect is humorous, for the appearance of the Green Knight has clearly not been a Christmas game. The light-hearted touches Birtwistle introduces into the opera – this example of irony, the war cry on its first appearance, the neighing of the Green Knight's horse, the clip-clop of its hooves – compensate to a certain degree for the absence in the work of the original poem's lightness of manner.

In a later article† Rhian Samuel draws attention to a motif that has much more important dramatic significance:

Gawain's name is marked by the pitches (G)–B♭–G♭ at significant points. [The motif's] first unmistakable appearance is when the Green Knight asks Gawain his name. It also occurs when Gawain identifies himself to Bertilak, and it illuminates the development of Gawain's character. The Green Knight sings these pitches several times, for

---

* The empty fifth, B–F♯, relates this to the Tarnhelm motif in *The Ring*.
† Rhian Samuel, 'Birtwistle's *Gawain*: An essay and a diary', *Cambridge Opera Journal*, vol.4, no.2 (1992), pp. 163–78.

instance, when Gawain has decapitated him; in his 'Ride north' aria ('madmen who know only one word – your name'); when he leaves Arthur's court; and when he calls Gawain to account in the second act. Further, the 'lulla' refrain of Morgan's lullaby in the Seduction scene starts with the rising figure G–B♭–G♭ in reference to the (thus far) hero. But after the Green Knight has wielded the axe, the name is no longer accompanied by true pitches. In fact, when Gawain returns to the court to be greeted by name by the assembled company, only the Fool achieves – just about – the right pitches. Thus confirming Gawain's protestation, 'I'm not that hero'.

In the opera Birtwistle's occasional touches of humour derive mainly from the Christmas pantomime. His sometimes bizarre manipulations of time, on the other hand, are closer to the surrealist theatre of Antonin Artaud than anything in the British tradition. When he sets the passing of the year against the time taken to strip, wash and arm Gawain for his journey, or when he inserts blackouts to indicate that he is cutting from one short span of time to another during the journey, we all understand that, although unusual, they are simply ways of conveying a long period of time in the theatre. But when he jumps back into the past as when Gawain lifts the axe and we go through the events leading up to the Green Knight's arrival again, or when he jumps into the future and we hear the knocking on the door and witness its opening and closing long before the actual arrival, or when Morgan tells Gawain about the journey before it has started, or when Bertilak and his wife welcome him when he is still in the process of travelling, he lifts the manipulation of time into the surreal. Although they were instigated to create dramatic tension, in the long run they give the impression that as well as being a spiritual allegory and a psychological drama, *Gawain* could well be the dream-like fantasy of the person who opens and closes the opera, and who thinks of herself as being all-knowing, all-seeing and in absolute control.

But perhaps the most striking thing about the opera is that although large sections of it are cyclic in construction and it contains these unexpected and sometimes disruptive time-shifts, its music always appears to be in a state of organic growth, it never ceases to press forward. In *The Mask of Orpheus* and *Yan Tan Tethera*, Birtwistle had to include orchestral substructures to achieve this condition. Here the forward momentum comes both from the melodic line itself and the impetus created by the layering of the orchestral music which shadows it. At every stage, even when the texture has to change in order to define the form of the music, there is at least one layer that has still to run its course. Consequently, like Wagner, Birtwistle is able to create structures of considerable length and define long stretches of time without any slackening of tension. As Peter Heyworth said in his review of the opera in the *Observer*: 'His music takes possession of the action (instead of merely illustrating it) to an extent that few, if any living composers can rival.'

Shortly after its first performance, Elgar Howarth, with Birtwistle's approval, arranged some of *Gawain*'s music into a concert piece. His models were Berg's 'Three Fragments from *Wozzeck*' and 'Five Symphonic Pieces from *Lulu*', works compiled to stimulate interest in the respective operas. Howarth hoped that his arrangement might whet the appetite of managers of other opera houses. He also thought it would interest conductors who wanted an attractive alternative to *The Triumph of Time*. Being a purely orchestral piece, the music of *Gawain's Journey* (83) jumps from one episode to another with instruments playing the vocal lines. It starts with the opening of the opera up until when Lady de Hautdesert begins her solo (three bars after figure 3), then moves to the entrance of the Green Knight and his challenge. Following this it goes back to when the court becomes visible after the opening duet for Morgan and Lady de Hautdesert, and then jumps forward to the beheading of the

Green Knight. From the second act Howarth selected first Morgan's lullaby then the three visions of the hunt interspersed with a section from the seduction of Gawain and the whole of the orchestra's version of Gawain's journey. The climax of the work is the killing of the fox. To round it off Howarth takes from when Morgan makes her final exit and we hear the sound of birdsong.

In fact the opera has not had another production to date. But it was revived by Covent Garden in 1994 and for this Birtwistle rewrote the masque so that it became half its original length and made a cut in the final scene. His reason for shortening the masque was simply because he felt there was too long a gap between the end of the real action in Act One (i.e., the exit of the Green Knight) and the beginning of Act Two. But it did mean that the off-stage chorus has to be cut out, the four Marian antiphons had to be replaced by sections of the 'Dies Irae', the six verses in which Gawain 'dreams his enemy' removed and most of the duet for Morgan and Lady de Hautdesert eliminated. As a consequence some of the score's richest music had to be scrapped.

The reason for the cut in the final scene between figure 150 and figure 174 was because this section brought back music jettisoned in the masque. This meant that the insights of Guinevere and the Fool into the probability that under the influence of Gawain the Knights of the Round Table could no longer remain 'beardless boys with nice suits of armour and a tiresome liking for male bonding' – as Harsent puts it but were bound to change. For Harsent this was a serious omission because it removed something of importance in his text. Unfortunately for him the damage will never be repaired, for it will be the much tighter revised version which will be performed when the opera is next produced. It has Birtwistle's seal of approval.

3
1992–1998

When Birtwistle received the coveted Ernst von Siemen's Music Prize in 1995, the event was marked by a concert given in the Prince Regent Theatre, Munich by Håkan Hardenberger and the Munich Chamber Orchestra under Mario Venzago. The two items in the programme were *Secret Theatre* and *Endless Parade* but, before the music began, Tom Phillips delivered a poetic tribute to the composer, and Birtwistle responded with an impromptu speech of thanks. It was mainly devoted to what he had been saying to the German press during the five preceding days.

'Two questions cropped up this week,' he said. 'One of them was "What did I think about the prize, and what did I think when I got it?" And the other one, which was more of a discussion, was "Did I know that my music was English?". Now the one thing that I rejected in my life was English music. I did it really from arrogance as a young man but it was a conscious thing. So I've never really thought of myself as an English composer.'*

'I seem to remember my father saying that you judge a prize by its pedigree, i.e. who else won it. So I was sent from your good people, from Siemens, a list of the people who'd won it and that really was a surprise, because here was the music establishment and there again I've never really considered myself to be part of the music establishment . . .'

Most people would find it hard to define English music.

* Hans-Theodor Wohlfahrt, ' "Ich weiss nicht, was englishe Musik ist." Eine Begegnung mit Harrison Birtwistle', *Neue Züricher Zeitung* (Frietag, 21 July 1995).

Robert Donington* thought it stemmed from 'our English flair for reconciliation', and among the many examples he cited was the way Dunstable reconciled 'a traditional British skill in sixths and thirds and six-four chords with the massive technique of the central schools'. He then listed the reconciliations of native tradition and continental innovations that characterized the music of English composers right through to Purcell. As an addendum to his article he drew attention to the music of Britten and Tippett. For them the continental influence was that of Stravinsky. Britten combined this with his indebtedness to Purcell and Schubert, Tippett with his fascination for the Elizabethan and Jacobean madrigalists and Beethoven. Notwithstanding his denial, Birtwistle too belongs to this tradition. His music is based on the combination of aspects of what he admired in works such as Stravinsky's *Agon*, Boulez's *Le marteau sans maître* and Stockhausen's *Zeitmasse* with medieval techniques. Where he differs from other English composers is that he has drawn on a much older tradition than anyone else, for some of the medieval techniques he uses, notably *cantus firmus* and *organum*, had their origins in the eleventh century.

Similarly the way he composes is typically English. He is governed not by theory, as his avant-garde colleagues on the continent tended to be in the fifties and sixties when he was moulding his style, but by practical experiment. This relates him to the long tradition of English empiricism. I think he would argue that he had been an empiricist long before he began paying homage to 'the sanctity of the context' in the early eighties. When he said he composed his first work, *Refrains and Choruses,* 'from the top of his head,' he meant that virtually for the first time he had been able to rid himself of the restraints which had impeded him as a composer during his student years. He cast aside theory, and simply got down to writing the piece as it came into his mind, his only criterion being 'will it work?'. The pre-compositional plans

* Robert Donington, 'Our English Flair for Reconciliation', *The Score*, March 1955, p.5.

he used in subsequent pieces were frequently crutches which could be abandoned once the work was under way. I now believe that *La Plage* was the exception rather than the rule.

When he referred to English music in Munich he was thinking mainly of composers such as Vaughan Williams, Delius and Holst, composers who were attempting to forge a national style through their use of folksong and the English pastoral tradition. Most composers of Birtwistle's generation, however, rejected this parochialism, and in any case Birtwistle grew up in an environment where the English pastoral tradition meant nothing. He and his colleagues in the Manchester School during the fifties, Peter Maxwell Davies and Alexander Goehr, selected Schoenberg, Webern, Stravinsky and Messiaen to be their mentors. Nevertheless later, when Birtwistle composed music for the theatre, he directed his attention to an English audience. He failed to take into account that one day he might want his work to travel abroad. 'In the case of *Punch and Judy*,' he once told me, 'I wanted a theatrical event that at one and the same time was very formal, a myth and English. The subject I eventually selected had the advantage of having a story everyone knew so that it wouldn't distract people from understanding what I was really trying to say.' Those from other parts of the world, however, would not have this advantage, and this may be one of the reasons why his theatrical pieces have been neglected overseas. Since composing *Gawain* (81), he has moved away from these specifically English topics. *Pulse Shadows* (101) received its first performance in Witten where it was sung in German; *The Second Mrs Kong* (90) has a plot which could take place anywhere; the episodes in the City of London could easily be situated in another venue. Within two years of its première at Glyndebourne in 1994 it had productions in Heidelberg and Vienna. Recently Birtwistle has been invited to become composer-in-residence to the Berlin Philharmonic Orchestra in succession to György Kurtág, an invitation that means he has achieved the pinnacle of international recognition. If he accepts the invitation he will have to write a major piece for the orchestra and accept that in future all his theatrical works will have to appeal to a world-wide audience from the outset.

Birtwistle prides himself on being an outsider who goes his own way whether in music or society. Although he may resent being included in the musical establishment, he cannot escape the fact that this is where he has been placed, especially by young composers. Indeed the important appointments he has been given in Britain since 1992 have required him to sell his house in France and move to a flat on the Isle of Dogs and a house in Wiltshire. In 1992 he was invited to join the board of the South Bank Centre. The following year, the London Philharmonic Orchestra made him their composer-in-residence. In this capacity he has been involved mainly in organizing concerts and workshops for children and young people. (*The Cry of Anubis* [93] was composed for one of them). That same year the post of Henry Purcell Chair in Composition at King's College, London was created for him. Later, in 1997, he became Director of Composition at the Royal Academy of Music as well. In 1993 he was Sue Lawley's guest on *Desert Island Discs*. The following year he wrote a work for the last night of the Proms which had an estimated audience on radio and television of a hundred million. Then, in the spring of 1996, a special three-week long festival of his music was given on the South Bank under the title 'Secret Theatres'.

Many young composers and musicians regard Birtwistle's music as old-fashioned. Like Boulez he has not abandoned the uncompromising principles he adopted in the fifties; he has not wanted to simplify his style or make his music immediately accessible as so many of his contemporaries have done in recent times. He utterly rejects post-modernism. When *Gawain* was revived at Covent Garden in April 1994, two young musicians who dubbed themselves The Hecklers, Frederick Stocken and Keith Burnstein, lovers of Wagner and advocates of 'good tunes', staged a demonstration at the close of the performance on the first night and went on to hold a press conference in the street outside. The stunt was said to have been organized by the *Evening Standard*, who were

having a running battle with the Royal Opera and wanted ammu-
nition for its fight. In the event the 'boos' of the two young men
were drowned by the applause in favour of the opera led by Lord
Gowrie, the chairman of the Arts Council. Typically Birtwistle
shrugged his shoulders and appeared to be indifferent to the opposition. But when he composed *Panic* (94) for the last night of the
Proms the following year to showers of abuse from the popular
press, it might have seemed that he had deliberately taken the
most extreme modernist stance in defiance of recent trends. He
claims that this was not so. He says he had wanted to write a work
for the saxophonist John Harle long before he received the
commission from the BBC. 'And if you know John,' he says, 'you'll
know why I had to write the kind of piece I did for him.'

The Second Mrs Kong, Birtwistle's fourth full-scale opera, is
essentially a comedy, although like all good comedies it has
deeply serious overtones. He received the commission from
Glyndebourne when *Gawain* was being rehearsed in spring 1991.
Glyndebourne wanted it for its main 1995 festival season, but to
obtain an Arts Council grant, the commission had to be for
Glyndebourne Touring Opera so that it had its initial run on tour
the year before. This meant that its forces had to be relatively
modest – an orchestra of sixty-six compared to the eighty-two
needed for *Gawain*, for instance. (The Heidelberg production
actually did it with considerably fewer.)

Birtwistle knew immediately that he wanted the new work to be
based on a modern myth, and he asked Russell Hoban to write the
libretto on the suggestion of Omar Ebrahim, who was playing the
Fool in *Gawain*. In the main Hoban's novels are about lonely
people who are unsure of their identity and live in a fantasy world
where they constantly reach out or search for something that eludes
them. On Ebrahim's advice Birtwistle read Hoban's *The Medusa
Frequency*,* an amusing, frequently surreal story about a novelist

* Russell Hoban, *The Medusa Frequency*, Jonathan Cape, London 1987;
Picador, London 1988.

who sits at his computer surrounded by reproductions of Vermeer's *Girl with a Pearl Earring*. To cure him of writer's block he has electrodes attached to his head, and these lead him 'to those places in your head that you can't get to on your own'. Among the various characters he meets on his bizarre journeys through the streets of London is the talking head of Orpheus. The only stipulation Birtwistle made when Hoban accepted the invitation to collaborate with him was that the opera should include a computer.

In the event Hoban drew on several of the characters and situations he had written about in *Turtle Diary* as well as *The Medusa Frequency*. *Turtle Diary*,* for example, contains an account of the film *King Kong* and its making in 1933. In essence *The Second Mrs Kong* is a modern version of the Orpheus myth, except that it begins in Hades and in order to find his Eurydice, the girl with the pearl earring, Kong has to ascend into the real world rather than the other way round. Once again Birtwistle wanted a director to be appointed early in the proceedings, and once again Peter Sellars was approached and then rejected for more or less the same reasons as before. In this instance, however, there was no delay in finding someone ideal for the job in Tom Cairns, whose advice and editorial skills proved to be invaluable. Birtwistle started composing the music as soon as he received the script for the first act, and when he began composing the second Hoban was only a week or two ahead of him.

The Second Mrs Kong was the last of Birtwistle's works to be published by Universal Edition. He had been with them since 1958, and they had always been enormously supportive of him. But in 1991 financial pressures meant that they had to dismiss most of the British composers on their books. Among his sketches for *Four Poems by Jaan Kaplinsky* dating from April of that year is a draft of the letter Birtwistle sent the Managing Director of Universal Edition in Vienna complaining of the

---

* Russell Hoban, *Turtle Diary*, Jonathan Cape, London 1975; Picador, London 1977.

high-handed manner of the firm's action. He was particularly incensed by the dismissal from their list of Simon Holt ('a young composer of considerable talent – ask Boulez or Berio'), and the way Vienna had overruled the advice of William Colleran who was in charge of the London branch.

Four years later when Universal Edition closed its London showroom and retained only a skeleton staff to run its operations in nearby Schotts, Birtwistle joined Boosey and Hawkes.

ANTIPHONIES

When Birtwistle received the joint commission from Vincent Meyer on behalf of the Philharmonia Orchestra and Betty Freeman on behalf of the Los Angeles Philharmonic to write a major piece for piano and orchestra, he hoped that either Barenboim or Brendel might be the soloist. Both were keen admirers of his work, indeed Brendel was even more enthusiastic about *Gawain* than he had been about *The Mask of Orpheus*. He attended every performance – 'How could I have kept away from such a masterpiece?' he said. But neither he nor Barenboim was free on the dates scheduled for the premières in Europe and America, so the engagements were secured by Mitsuko Uchida. She gave the first American performance with the Los Angeles Philharmonic in May 1996, but illness prevented her from being the soloist at the European première in May 1993. This was undertaken by Joanna MacGregor, who mastered the work's formidable difficulties in a matter of weeks.

As it happened Birtwistle had no specific pianist in mind when composing *Antiphonies* (86). In this instance it was not the personality of the performer that concerned him, it was the nature of the instrument and its relationship with the orchestra accompanying it. The volume of notes it can produce at any one time, its range and its sheer physical power, means that the piano is the only instrument which can match an orchestra on more or less equal terms. It is therefore ideally suited to respond to it antiphonally. What it lacks is the orchestra's variety of colour and ability to sustain notes. It may be able to create the illusion that notes are being sustained in a cantabile line, but nevertheless each note begins to fade as soon as it is struck. Birtwistle has never wanted to disguise this fact. He treats the piano as a highly versatile, tuned percussion instrument, which is precisely what it is. Apart from two pieces designed for children (*Sad Song* and *Berceuse de Jeanne*), the only time he uses the piano to sustain a line is in one or two of the arias in *La Plage*, but even there its main function is to supply the sound of the fading bell. For him the piano is not a *cantus* instrument. This means that *Antiphonies* is basically different from all previous works for piano and orchestra in that the pianist never has a 'singing' tune. When he does ask for a passage to be played cantabile, it is for those kinds of ethereal textures Schumann and Chopin developed by means of the sustaining pedal. Essentially they are textures compounded from multiple arabesques. This one comes from the second main section of *Antiphonies*.

Structurally *Antiphonies* consists of an introduction and a coda framing five sections of unequal length. Each section begins with one of these arabesque-like textures on the piano and proceeds to a situation where its capacity to be highly percussive predominates. At such times piano and orchestra become deeply opposed to each other in their alternations. But the overall purpose of the music is to reach a situation where the two become reconciled. The turning point occurs near the end of the fifth section when the antiphony between the piano playing highly percussive music with the two harps is set against a very simple chorale in the upper woodwind. Until then the orchestra's *cantus* line has been either too high or too low to be followed as a melody without difficulty. But after this chorale it moves down to the middle register and its intervals become narrow enough to be followed with ease. As it begins to fade away, the piano plays the last of its arabesque passages, but this time a flute picks out and sustains some of its notes to make a tune out of them. The final gesture of reconciliation comes when the piano alternates with glockenspiel, crotales, vibraphone, tubular bells and the two harps so that the mighty chords they produce sound like two great bells responding to each other harmoniously.

As in *Endless Parade*, most of the material has its origins in the work's introductory section, except that here it is less vivid than in the trumpet piece and more embryonic. Most of the growth takes place in the highly dramatic first section, the essence of the drama being the conflict between lyrical and percussive material. In the part leading up to the climax of the first section, the much more aggressive percussive material wins out. Afterwards lyricism prevails and the percussive material loses its dynamism. At first (beginning on page 2 of the full score) the piano's lyrical arabesques alternate with a percussive passage precipitated by a 'savage' three-note gesture on the trombones. Their assertiveness suggests that the piano should abandon its lyrical manner and fall in line with them. When it does, the soloist's aggression bears down on lyrical ideas that have appeared on cor anglais and tuba. The situation is only resolved after the piano has been momentarily silenced by the banter of antiphonal exchanges taking place within the orchestra. It resumes its activity after the music has wound down and lyricism returns with a passage on muted tuba. The soloist's last gesture is a series of staccatissimo chords devoid of assertiveness. All is ready for a new dramatic cycle to begin its course.

Antiphonies lasts nearly thirty-five minutes and during that time the soloist hardly stops playing. Although it contains some extraordinary moments such as some highly imaginative bell-like sonorities, a whiff of syncopated jazz, a delightfully witty scherzo and an amusing passage which sounds like the clip-clop of the Green Knight's horse, it lacks the sweep of *Melencolia 1* and the variety of *Endless Parade*. This is almost certainly because Birtwistle wanted to steer as far away as possible from what the traditional piano concerto had been. He not only denies the soloist sustained melodies, he also provides no opportunities for display. Even so the work does have roots in the past. They lie in those piano trios, quartets and quintets of Haydn, Mozart, Beethoven, Schubert and Brahms in which the piano is also always on the go. The formidable difficulties Birtwistle poses for the soloist are therefore not just technical, the passages of rapid antiphonal exchange involve the timing and rapport with colleagues the skilled chamber musician requires.

FIVE DISTANCES

Immediately after completing *Antiphonies* Birtwistle began work on a wind quintet for the virtuoso players of the Ensemble InterContemporain in which timing and rapport with colleagues are taken to an extreme. For instance, in the passage which heralds the closure of the work (five bars after figure 25) the flute, oboe and clarinet each play highly flexible, independent melodies fluctuating by means of accelerandos and rallentandos between quaver = 72 and quaver = 96. Since they enter one after the other, the flute has to cue the oboe's entrance, and the oboe the clarinet's. Beneath them the horn and bassoon play metrically strict ostinatos at a tempo of quaver = 128, but to coordinate with the flute, oboe and clarinet they have to pause every so often and wait for a cue from one of them before they can proceed. To make things even more difficult for the players, they have to sit as far apart from each other as is practically possible. On the score's title page, Birtwistle suggests that they sit in a wide semicircle with the horn centre back and the flute and oboe at the front and at opposite sides of the platform. This has the advantage of making the lines clear in performance, but throughout the piece the players have to be acutely aware of the fluctuations in tempo and perpetually on the alert as to where their cues are coming from and how to coordinate with their colleagues.*

Five Distances for Five Players (87) also makes extensive use of antiphony, except that five instruments cannot be divided into alternating 'choirs' answering each other with the same type of material, they have to create the illusion of antiphony by alternating contrasting material. The basic contrast is between lyrical passages and those in which rhythm is paramount. The lyrical passages tend to be metrically fluid, legato and fairly slow, the rhythmic ones metrically strict, staccato and fairly fast. As in *Antiphonies* the alternation between them always results in the rhythmically orientated passages having the last word. In the passage cited above, for instance, the flute, oboe and clarinet eventually abandon their lyrical individualism to play a fast, metrically strict phrase in rhythmical unison. In other words, a section which began with these instruments being independent of each other ends with them becoming a unified chorus despite the physical distance between them.

* In *Five Distances for Five Players* Birtwistle was acknowledging his debt to Stockhausen's *Zeitmasse* and *Gruppen*, which were so important to him when he was a student struggling to find his voice. *Zeitmasse* is a wind quintet which exploits the simultaneous use of different tempos, some strict, some free; *Gruppen*, a work for three orchestras, employs distance to clarify the complex polyphony created by textures moving at different speeds.

Structurally this is the essence of the work. Similar transformations occur in those sections where the cantus is transformed into a rhythmic continuum as in *Secret Theatre*. One notable example is the section leading up to the climax of the work which occurs when flute, oboe, clarinet and bassoon arrive at a stage of common accord (six before figure 21). As might be expected, the section starts with these instruments playing independent material, the flute and clarinet having highly embellished lyrical lines, the oboe and bassoon rhythmic ostinatos essentially staccato in character (figure 17). The transformation occurs when the flute and clarinet are pulled into the much simpler, more focused ostinatos so that all four instruments play the same type of material and can begin hocketing with each other before becoming a unified chorus. At one stage they even hocket with the horn, which until then has pursued its own course.

On the grounds that it is the only brass instrument in the ensemble, the role of the horn throughout the piece is, as it had been in *Refrains and Choruses*, that of odd-man-out. But whereas in the earlier piece this only became evident after the occurrence of the perfectly symmetrical chord about halfway through the work, here the role is clear from the outset. The repetition of its gruff fanfares leave us in no doubt that it is going to take its independence to an extreme. Indeed, it is this which provides the work with most of its tension. There are just two occasions when it becomes more or less at one with its colleagues. The first is when all five players have to play three staccato chords together (figure 16), the other when the work peters out like some clockwork machine winding down, and all five players become involved in the process.

THREE SETTINGS OF CELAN

As well as completing *Antiphonies* and writing *Five Distances* in the summer of 1992, Birtwistle composed two more Celan settings for the same forces as *White and Light* (soprano, two clarinets, viola, cello and double bass), thus making a group of three for Mary Wiegold and the Composers Ensemble to perform under his direction in the early autumn. The new ones were Michael Hamburger's translations of *Nacht* and *Tenebrae*.

'Tenebrae' was composed first but placed last in the group. Celan got the idea for the poem from Couperin's *Leçons de Ténèbres*, a setting of the Lamentations of Jeremiah, 'Judaism's principal elegy for the fall of Jerusalem and all subsequent misfortunes'.* In the Roman Catholic tradition *tenebrae* were formerly the offices of matins and lauds that take place during the night on the Thursday, Friday and Saturday of Holy Week, when the candles were extinguished one by one and everything became shrouded in darkness. Celan also included references to the Holocaust in his poem, but details of this were not available until John Felstiner published his literary biography of the poet in 1995. For instance, we now know that among other things the lines 'Handled already, Lord, / clawed and clawing as though / the body of each of us were / your body, Lord', refer to Jews clawing with their fingernails at the door of the gas chamber in Auschwitz. Birtwistle used Michael Hamburger's early translation which in the fourth stanza differs from the one in the new 1995 edition of his translations.† Instead of 'Wind-awry we went there, / went there to bend / over hollow and ditch', the new translation reads: 'Askew we went there, / went there to bend / down to the trough, to the crater.'

Birtwistle's response to a poem about a group of people going to their deaths and crying to their Lord to pray for them was to cast his song as a scena. Throughout, the viola, supported by cello and double bass, suggests the heavy tread of feet stumbling slowly onward, the pace quickening only when the end is in sight: 'Pray, Lord. / We are near.' The word 'Lord' occurs

---

* John Felstiner, *Paul Celan – Poet, Survivor, Jew*, Yale University Press, 1995, p.101.
† *Poems of Paul Celan*, translated by Michael Hamburger, Anvil Press, London 1995.

eleven times and falls either in the middle or at the end of a sentence: ' We are near, Lord, / near and at hand' or ' It was blood, it was / what you shed, Lord.' To give it emphasis Celan always precedes it with a comma. Birtwistle follows suit with a rest.

Although the song belongs to the category he calls 'horizontal music' (melodic development), his sketches reveal that on several occasions he worked out the rhythm of the vocal line first, particularly when the anacrusis to 'Lord' needs to be articulated rapidly in order to convey a sense of urgency, i.e: 'It cast your image into our eyes, Lord. / Our eyes and our mouths are so open and empty, Lord. / We have drunk, Lord. / The blood and the image that was in the blood, Lord.' Although difficult to confirm owing to the paucity of sketches for his vocal lines, in all probability working out the rhythm first is his usual procedure when setting words.

He obtained the pitch from two symmetrically ordered scales lying a fifth apart.

'Lord' is always sung on E and given additional emphasis by a scurrying elaboration of it by the two clarinets which, as in *White and Light* and indeed all his Celan settings, shadow the singer throughout the song. When the text before and after it is short

Birtwistle draws the notes from the upper scale, but for variety, and when the text is longer, he dips down into the lower one. On one occasion, for the words 'It gleamed', he transposes notes from the lower one up an octave to convey not only brightness but also a shriek of horror.

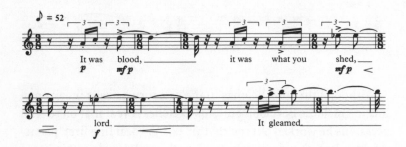

The orientation of this line around two fifths, A–E–B, has a direct bearing on the constant references throughout the sketches to the open strings of the viola, cello and double bass. In the main these instruments are given double stops to play, and double stops sound much more effective, much more 'ringing', if an open string is involved. In his sketch for the chords the cello and viola have to play after 'It gleamed', he writes out the notes of their open strings as a reminder. For the viola he uses the bass and treble clefs.

The Mask of Orpheus, English National Opera, May 1986.
Birtwistle with Eurydice (Jean Rigby)
in front of the mask of Orpheus *(Zoë Dominic)*

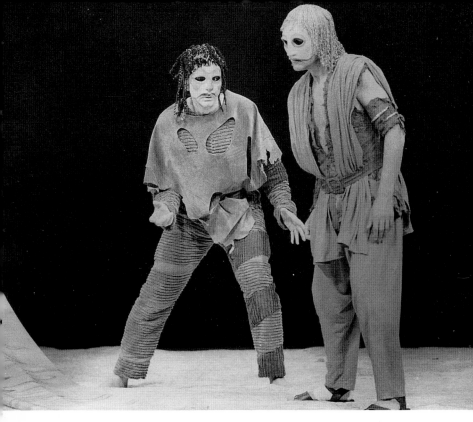

(*Above*) *The Mask of Orpheus*, English National Opera, May 1986.
Aristaeus (Tom McDonnel) and Orpheus (Philip Langridge) (*Zoë Dominic*)
(*Below*) The death of Orpheus at the hands of the Maenads (*Zoë Dominic*)

Harrison Birtwistle (*right*) with David Harsent,
Gawain's librettist (*Simon Harsent*)

The Second Mrs Kong, Glyndebourne, October 1994.
Pearl (Helen Field) at her computer with the head of King Kong
from the RKO film on her computer screen behind *(Guy Gravett)*

The Second Mrs Kong, Glyndebourne, October 1994.
Kong (Philip Langridge) and Orpheus (Michael Chance) *(above)*
outside a telephone box in a bad part of town *(Guy Gravett)*
Kong and Pearl *(below)* 'together and apart for ever' *(Guy Gravett)*

Harrison Birtwistle in Wiltshire *(above)* in January 1997
and *(below)* in May 1997 *(Betty Freeman/Lebrecht Collection)*

As in the *Four Songs of Autumn*, a harmonic framework of fifths is combined with symmetrically ordered scales in such a way that there is little or no opposition between them. The soprano's constant return to E and her extension up to B when she sings 'It gleamed' relates unmistakably to the viola's D–A–E.

The reiteration of a specific note as a point of reference is also characteristic of Birtwistle's setting of *Night*. He selected this poem mainly because 'night and darkness' contrast well with 'white and light'. However, it is one of Celan's most obscure poems. Its inner meaning only becomes evident if the reader knows (or guesses) that when Celan refers to 'eyes' he means the eyes that 'gaze from or at the Jewish dead',* and that he likens the eyes of the dead to stones or pebbles.

> Pebbles and scree. And a shard note, thin,
> as the hour's message of comfort.
>
> Exchange of eyes, finite, at the wrong time:
> image-constant,
> lignified
> the retina-:
> the sign of eternity.
>
> Conceivable:
> up there, in the cosmic network of rails,
> like stars,
> the red of two mouths.
>
> Audible (before dawn): a stone
> that made the other its target.†

Birtwistle divides his song into three sections, ABA – B being his setting of the second stanza. He draws most of his musical imagery from 'And a shard note, thin, as the hour's message of

* Felstiner, p. 86.
† Reprinted by permission of Anvil Press Poetry.

comfort'. In both the first and last sections, the clarinets reiterate slowly and softly a falling ninth (C–B) to convey 'the hour's message of comfort' For the 'shard note', he has the viola play throughout the song short fragments of two or three notes staccato, and for the notion of thinness he asks the soprano to sing 'scree' on a high G and to continue to sing in a high register until she reaches ' the red of two mouths', where she has to echo the comforting (and comfortable) falling ninth the clarinets have been playing in their middle register. The principal musical image in the contrasting B section stems from 'lignified the retina', and to represent the eyes of the dead the soprano's line is broken up by rests to produce a stiff, stilted effect.

Celan has been accused of 'aestheticizing' the events in the death camps. But as Michael Hamburger points out in reference to *Todesfuge*, Celan's most famous and widely anthologized poem, 'the power of the poem arises from the extreme tension between its grossly impure material and its almost pure form . . . the personal anguish is transposed into distancing imagery and a musical structure so intricate that a "terrible beauty" is wrested from the ugly theme.'* I think Birtwistle could also be accused of 'aestheticizing': *White and Light*, *Night* and *Tenebrae* are some of the most lyrical and engaging pieces he has composed. Even when the soprano has to sing in a stiff, stilted manner in *Night* or focus on rapid rhythmical articulation in *Tenebrae*, an instrument supplies the lyricism in a line moving in counterpoint with her. To provide the music which would expose the 'dark' side of Celan's imagery, he had to alternate the songs with movements for string quartet.

* Hamburger, 1972, op.cit., p. 12.

THREE MOVEMENTS FOR STRING QUARTET

The notion that his Celan settings might ultimately be juxta-posed with instrumental music of a much tougher nature had occurred to Birtwistle when he was writing *Four Poems of Jaan Kaplinski* (82) in 1991. It became more of a possibility in 1993 when he composed for the Arditti Quartet two *Fantasias* to go with the *Frieze* he had written earlier. Eventually these *Three Movements for String Quartet* (89) were incorporated into *Pulse Shadows* (101) where they appear as *Frieze 1, Fantasia 2* and *Fantasia 4*.

One of the features that links the songs and the instrumental movements is that all give prominence to the viola. But the simi-larities between the two groups are considerably less important than the contrasts, for, whereas the songs are essentially lyrical and depend on 'melodic development', the quartet pieces are based on 'rhythmic development'. The *Friezes*, other than the one Birtwistle composed in 1991, remain in the same tempo and metre throughout their course, and develop rhythmical figures without changing their basic characters; the *Fantasias*, on the other hand, fluctuate in tempo and metre, and transform rhyth-mical figures almost beyond recognition. They are closer to the English viol fantasias of the sixteenth and seventeenth centuries than to later keyboard models such as those of Bach, Mozart and Beethoven.

Even though they rapidly change moods and involve extreme contrasts, both *Fantasia 2* and *Fantasia 4* have clear-cut structures based on Birtwistle's usual procedure of going through the same events in different ways. *Fantasia 2* begins with a paragraph in which change of tempo and metre is paramount. It opens with flautando (flute-like) strokes played in the traditional seven-teenth-century imitative style immediately followed by an accelerando to a faster tempo where rhythmical unisons prevail and the music becomes almost jocose in character. After a momen-tary return to flautando, the paragraph ends by contrasting an assertive *fff* chord with delicate ones marked *ppp* and *pp* on either side of it. This paragraph is then expanded into two longer sections in which these ideas are developed, and particular attention is paid to accelerating from one tempo to another. The piece reaches its climax when soft flautando chords are set against short, aggressive ejaculations, the tempo accelerates to as fast as possible and the players are no longer required to synchronize with each other.

Fantasia 4 follows a similar plan, but here the first of its three sections is concerned with the transformation of a rhythmical unit consisting of a sustained chord followed by a rest and an extremely short *ppp* chord. Within a matter of seconds the sustained chord becomes a frenetic passage for viola, and the short *ppp* chord an explosive *ff*. As in *Fantasia 2* the following two sections develop these features, the most violent contrast occurring near the end when, before the last series of frenetic passages for the viola, the instrumentalists play undulating lines across at least three of their strings 'senza nuance' and with one finger only to create a particularly docile effect.

In *Pulse Shadows*, *Fantasia 2* comes immediately after *White and Light*, and although they have no intended bearing on each other, the accelerations in the instrumental piece, which eventually get out of hand and result in a free-for-all, appear to be a violent and disruptive version of the gentle accelerations in the song's drifting viola line. In other words, song and fantasia are linked to each at a much deeper level than the prominence of the viola.

THE SECOND MRS KONG

Birtwistle's theatrical works fall into two groups. On the one hand are the four full-length operas – *Punch and Judy*, *The Mask of Orpheus*, *Gawain* and *The Second Mrs Kong*; on the other are shorter works that, on the whole, require less elaborate staging and fewer resources – *Down by the Greenwood Side*, *Bow Down* and *Yan Tan Tethera*. To a greater or lesser degree, all seven contain, within the linear narrative, repetitive or cyclic events. This follows Birtwistle's compositional practice throughout his music in general. In the full-length operas the linear unfolding involves a journey undertaken by the principal character which culminates in the acquisition of self-knowledge. I believe this to be true even of Mr Punch. As well as this, the four operas also contain a character who controls or tries to control the action. This, I think, is a projection of how Birtwistle sees himself as a composer. He may use random numbers and give his performers freedom of choice from time to time, but he always insists that basically he is in control. In his operas, however, the degree of control depends on the nature of the work. In the 'serious' ones, those who pull the strings – Apollo in *The Mask of Orpheus* and Morgan in *Gawain* – have more or less absolute jurisdiction over events; in the 'comic' ones – Choregos in *Punch and Judy* and Anubis in *The Second Mrs Kong* – they are only nominally in charge, their unexpected lack of overall control being the turning point in the respective works.

Another feature Birtwistle's theatrical pieces share is an extremely arresting visual image or setting. This is true even of *Bow Down* where there is nothing on stage but five actors and four musicians sitting in a circle. But their choral breathing, drumbeats, oboe plaints, gently hummed chords and slow hieratic acting produce a surreal atmosphere that is directly in line with all Birtwistle's other works for the stage.

Nowhere is this surreal atmosphere more in evidence than in *The Second Mrs Kong* (90). The action takes place in four locations: an island in the world of shadows where the dead live, a stockbroker's hi-tech penthouse dominated by a huge computer screen, the interior of a sewer leading to the city, and a desolate street 'in a bad part of town'. The work bristles with humorous situations and dialogue. Even the list of characters is intended to give rise to a smile. The heroine is Pearl, Vermeer's *Girl with a Pearl Earring*, the hero King Kong, the ape in the 1933 film of that name, or rather the idea of Kong. Other characters from the world of films include Mr Dollarama, a dead film producer, his wife Inanna, a dead former beauty queen and Swami Zumzum, her dead lover and spiritual adviser. There are also mythological characters. As well as Eurydice and the Head of Orpheus, Russell Hoban has a substantial part for Anubis, the Egyptian deity with a human body and a jackal's head. It is he who transports the souls of the dead to the world of shadows in his boat.

In that the first act ends in a state of chaos and the second terminates when the hero and heroine have found each other at last, the opera is not unlike the comic opera structures that Rossini brought to perfection. However, it would be totally unlike either Hoban or Birtwistle to write anything comic that was not also deeply serious. In this sense *The Second Mrs Kong* is closer to Mozart's comic operas than to Rossini's. Pearl and Kong may eventually find each other, but when they ask the mirror on the wall to tell them whether this is the moment when their happiness begins it replies, 'No. This is the moment when reality begins. You cannot have each other.' They cannot even touch each other. All they have is their yearning. 'It is not love that moves the world from night to morning,' says the mirror, 'it is not love that makes the new day dawn. No. It is the longing for what cannot be.' The opera ends with Pearl and Kong calling 'I remember' to each other. But their memories of each other are severely limited. All they can possibly remember is that she said she loved him, and he said that his love for her was fifty feet high.

When it reaches this stage, the opera has turned full circle, for it begins with the dead going through some memory over and over again. At first we hear only fragments of the remembered lives. Then Vermeer is allowed to relive in full his memory of when he first met Pearl. But it is Kong, sitting in a corner watching the film *King Kong* on a projector, who in his opening words expresses the gist of the opera, at least as far as he is concerned: 'Who am I? What am I the idea of? What of me is real?' These questions may be trite, but in this instance Kong is more than justified in raising them. Russell Hoban tells us in the preface to his libretto: 'There never was a fifty-foot-high gorilla; there never was even a fifty-foot-high fake gorilla – only the idea is fifty feet high. The physical Kong of the RKO film was a creature of bits and pieces, chief among which were a giant head and shoulders, a giant hand and foot, and an eighteen-inch articulated model. The giant head rolled its eyes and opened and closed its jaws in sync with terrifying roars; the giant hand picked up Fay Wray; the giant foot stepped heavily on Skull Island extras; and the eighteen-inch model, moved by the hand of Willis O'Brien one-sixteenth of an inch at a time, climbed a scale-model Empire State Building in stop-motion photography.'

In the opera Kong first encounters Pearl when he hears her voice during Vermeer's memory of when he painted her. Pearl encounters Kong when she hears his voice in the background, and is told by the mirror that he is the king (the Kong) 'who sits in the shadows of the future'. In the future, of course, reproductions of the painting of Pearl can be seen everywhere including a stockbroker's penthouse in the City of London. It is from there that Pearl calls up Kong on a computer and they fall in love. She wants him alive and tells him that in the film the death he saw was not his death, 'What you are cannot die!' This is something he has yet to discover for himself, but in the meantime they arrange to meet 'where the city types live'. On his journey there, he is accompanied by the Head of Orpheus. In hot pursuit of them are Anubis and the dead. Anubis also plays the role of the Death of Kong and in a desolate street in a bad part of town Kong and the Death of Kong confront each other. The Death of Kong says, 'The movie is the story and you can't fool with the story.' Kong died, he claims, when the aeroplanes shot him down from the Empire State Building. Kong points out that there never was a giant ape. 'I'm the idea of Kong. What I am cannot die.' Kong has at last discovered for himself what he truly is. They fight and the Death of Kong perishes. Kong then finds Pearl in the penthouse. It is the first time they have actually met, yet they cannot even touch each other. As the mirror tells them, they are doomed to be 'together and apart for ever'.

The opera is cast in two acts each with four scenes. But another way of regarding the overall structure is to see it as an introduction followed by three large substructures each culminating in a duet for Kong and Pearl. The last of these involves the journey Kong must take from the world of shadows to the penthouse in the city. It starts at the end of the first act and continues right up to the last scene of the second. What characterizes these substructures is that all three are taken up with linear development. Virtually the only cyclic event of any significance in the opera occurs in the introduction where its purpose, at least on the surface, is to promote humour.

The introduction opens with a two-part 'aria' for Anubis, which establishes his occupation, character and position as master of ceremonies. It is on his instructions that the dead repetitively go through fragments of their remembered lives. The cycle of Inanna and Zumzum coupling on their rumpled bed, Dollarama shooting them and then being shot by Inanna, of Vermeer seeing Pearl for the first time, of Eurydice reaching out to Orpheus and Orpheus crying out for her, occurs four times. On each successive occasion the sequence becomes shorter and more nonsensical. But the import of what they remember is yearning. Inanna longs to be loved by someone she can love; Vermeer longs to see 'a face like music'; Orpheus and Eurydice long to find each other. Eventually in the second act Inanna's yearning finds expression in one of the most moving episodes in the opera.

It is Vermeer's yearning that opens the first of the substructures. Birtwistle casts it in the form of an ecstatic 'aria' for him sung in the 'Place of Memory'. At the same time in the 'World of Shadows', a monstrous messenger delivers a print of *King Kong* to Kong, and Inanna, Dollarama, Zumzum and Anubis supply the background to Kong's presence in the underworld. Vermeer then remembers the four women who offer themselves as models for him. When Pearl appears and is chosen, the separation of the 'Place of Memory' (the past) and the 'World of Shadows' (the present) is eventually bridged, the coming together occurring when Pearl and Kong sing their duet. To his 'Lost and lonely in the shadows', she replies '. . . waits a Kong who never was'.

Before the second substructure gets under way, Inanna makes advances to Kong, and he tells her about the voice that spoke to him. As in the first sub-structure, the second also takes place on two levels. On the first are Pearl and the mirror, on the second everything that appears on a huge computer screen in the penthouse where Pearl has found herself, including clips from *Brief Encounter, Night Train* and *King Kong*. Here the two levels are bridged when Pearl wallops her computer and Kong, sitting at his, appears on her screen. In their ensuing duet they declare their love and Kong promises to go to her penthouse.

Kong is able to make his escape from the World of Shadows when Dollarama and Zumzum quarrel and everything is thrown into chaos by a communal fight. Because it lasts nearly an hour, the third substructure has to be divided into sections. The first culminates in the reappearance of the four women from the first act now cast as the Four Temptations. Their words suggest that, like Inanna, they too yearn for Kong. So too does Madame Lena, the 'customary sphinx' who guards the exit to the world of the living. Hers is a comic role: 'I too have been waiting for you, I too, waiting in the desert silence, in the dry wind of my dream.' Eventually, when Kong and his companion, the Head of Orpheus, reach the city, they encounter Anubis in his role as the Death of Kong. After he has been killed, Inanna sings her deeply expressive, bluesy lament, accompanied by flute, alto saxophone, accordion and lower strings playing pizzicato: 'In all my life and all my death I've wanted something and it never happened, never, never, happened.' Her lament functions as a preparation for the final duet where Pearl and Kong repeat over and over again, 'You remember?' – 'I remember', their amplified voices fading away into the distance and becoming ever more separated.

Although Birtwistle's music can sometimes be humorous, as when he illustrates the shooting of Kong and his fall from the Empire State Building in the film clip that occurs in Act Two, for the most part it deals with the dark side of the plot. Hoban says he has never heard any music that conveys a sense of 'becoming' so strongly, and by this he means the feeling of 'reaching out' which is one of his main concerns in the libretto. For his part, Birtwistle says that the opera 'sits' on the thick texture of his score. His music supplies what the characters can only talk about. Not even in the poignantly beautiful final duet with its long pedal on a low E do we experience a sense of arrival or conclusion. The tension between the humour and surreal imagery of Hoban's libretto and the music Birtwistle provides for the orchestra (which often seems to be moving at a slower rate than the pace of the events taking place on stage) creates an atmosphere that makes *The Second Mrs Kong* both compelling and deeply disturbing.

The sketches for *The Mask of Orpheus* and *Gawain* contained in the Paul Sacher Foundation library are more or less complete. In contrast there are comparatively few for *The Second Mrs Kong* – 88 pages for a score covering 268 pages. Most of them are devoted to two or three episodes in the opera. From them it is difficult to find any evidence for Birtwistle's claim that the score is built primarily from whole-tone scales. Nor can their presence be verified by a visual perusal of the score. The verification comes only when one listens to the work. It is then that one becomes aware of the orientation to whole tones at certain prominent moments in the score. They provide a harmonic colour which overrides the usual tonal palate Birtwistle founds on fourths and fifths. However, the reason for this is hard to pinpoint in such a chromatic score. The only explanation is that the key phrase Pearl utters during the jumble of remembered lives just after the first act has got under way is 'Who are you?', and for this her notes are E–D–B♭. (The other three notes of the whole tone scale, C–A♭–G♭, are provided by the orchestra.)

The Swiss library does contain a folder of twelve-stave paper in which some of his 'pre-compositional' ideas are outlined in the form of sets of seven-note scales containing three tones and three semitones systematically arranged in different orders, and sets of four-note units similar to those contained in his sketches for *Four Poems by Jaan Kaplinski*. Those for the Kaplinski songs reveal his preoccupation with intervals (calculated in semitones) and the symmetries obtainable from them.

To turn these into a potential melody, Birtwistle selected four of the units (A2, B1, B3 and B4) and ordered them so that the lowest of the three pitch layers is focused exclusively on D, the highest moves from E to E♭ and back to E again, while the middle one has a melodic shape built from a five-note chromatic scale (G–A♭–A–B♭–B).

Birtwistle then supplied these notes with a rhythm based on permutations of durations lasting two, three and four semiquavers. But the result must have been too 'simplistic' to be of any use in the actual composition of the songs. It was clearly an abstract for a way of proceeding rather than a sketch for something specific. His setting of the lines 'Heart of rain where nothing stirs' illustrates the point.

Here the lowest of the three layers or lines also makes a melodic shape out of G–A♭–A–B♭–B, the highest focuses on B♭, while the middle uses E♭–E–G♭–F for its curve.

There are dozens of complex lines compounded from two or three layers such as this in *The Second Mrs Kong*. Birtwistle opens Vermeer's 'aria' in Act One with a phrase which also leaps from register to register. He directs it to be sung cantabile and 'trance-like'.

Before Hoban embarked on the libretto, Birtwistle had asked him whether he could provide each of the characters with a different speaking style. When this proved impossible, the onus fell on the composer to differentiate the characters by means of different singing styles. The line which swings from one octave to another with the use of falling minor sevenths and rising major sevenths is characteristic of Vermeer's 'ecstatic' style of utterance. Dollarama, the other baritone in the cast, delivers most of his lines in *sprechgesang*. Anubis, a bass-baritone with a slightly lower range, leaps from one layer to another in a mode which is not only illustrative of the words that introduce him

('The rocking and the swing of it'), but also suggests the wail that comes from his jackal's head and his agitated mode of behaviour in general.

The four-note sets in the folder of twelve-stave manuscript paper contained in the sketches for the opera do have some bearing on the melodic material, but not directly. The work contains a great many four-note phrases, as the orchestral introduction to Act One bears witness, but the only one that appears in the sets is the one used for Pearl's confession of love. In the sets the notes are C–D–G–A♭. Even though transposed and reordered versions of this unit characterize what Pearl sings, particularly at moments of significance in the first act, it would be a mistake to think of it as the opera's love motif. D–C–A♭ may well be the source of the notes E–D–B♭ she used for 'Who are you?' Her response to Vermeer's 'God in Heaven' can be considered a variant of the unit. Had it been intended as the opera's love motif the relationship between 'Hallelujah' and 'I love you' would have been obvious. It would have transcended the half-hour gap between the appearances.

THE CRY OF ANUBIS

Four-note units are even more prevalent in *The Cry of Anubis*, the work Birtwistle composed for an education concert given by the London Philharmonic Orchestra which he devised in his capacity as the orchestra's composer-in-residence. The work is for tuba and a symphony orchestra reduced to fit into the restricted space of the Queen Elizabeth Hall (double woodwind, four horns, two trumpets, timpani, percussion, harp and strings). In many ways it is the easiest of his pieces to follow for the structure falls into clearly defined sections, the repetitions can be recognized as repetitions and are not as varied as in his other music. The constant repetition of the note D in a low register means that it is harmonically much more rooted than usual, and at no time do the textures become opaque.

On the evidence of his previous three works for soloist and orchestra, Birtwistle first of all decides on the nature of the solo instrument, then on what its relationship with the accompanying orchestra could be. In particular he takes into account the areas in which the two will be able to interact. Finally he selects a drama for them to play out. As we have seen this can take various forms, but in the end whatever happens will inevitably end in reconciliation.

The tuba has a smooth, rich tone and is at its most beautiful when playing soft, legato phrases in its middle register. It can also be very agile, its flexibility enabling it to negotiate wide skips with ease. Its staccato notes can sound like double-bass pizzicatos when played softly; when played loudly they can match the power of a well-tuned set of pedal timpani. Since it requires an enormous amount of breath, long phrases are almost impossible to sustain. Birtwistle takes advantage of this by always presenting it in dialogue with instruments that occupy the same or part of the same register as it. This means that in *The Cry of Anubis* it rarely if ever plays anything without the assistance of another instrument. The work is therefore divided into a series of encounters with the tuba always endeavouring to come out on top, to be the instrument in charge of affairs. It is this which justifies the piece being called *The Cry of Anubis* for at no time does Birtwistle quote the actual cry of Anubis that occurs in the opera. Nor, apart from at the very beginning of the opera, is Anubis closely associated with the tuba. The title merely alludes to his attempts to be the boss.

The work opens with the tuba in dialogue with the viola section, but even though its soft, lyrical phrase lies in its best register, no player can sustain it without snatching a breath somewhere, and so it cannot rival the perfectly sustained line the violas can play. The soloist then turns to the double bass section. At first the basses merely shadow it and supply suitable notes to complete each of the tuba's three phrases (always F–E–B♭–D). Then a contest arises. They attempt to outdo each other in their agility to climb from a low register to a particularly high one. The tuba's next encounter is with the timpani, and it is here that the drama begins to take off in earnest. The two most significant events in the course of it are first, when the rivalry between tuba and timpani is subdued by the violins, violas and cellos authoritatively acting in unison, and secondly, when the two eventually unite in the playing of a percussive cadenza-like passage just before the end of the work. Their duet results in the most vigorous affirmation of the note D there has been until then. Against it the tuba wistfully recalls the lyrical, four-note phrase it reiterated before the build-up to the climax (D–C–D♭–B). The last word, however, goes to the tubular bells and harp reaffirming the D.

PANIC

Normally when Birtwistle writes a new work he likes it to be in a different medium from the one he has just completed. After an orchestral work he might choose to compose a song or some chamber music. *The Cry of Anubis* was followed by *Hoquetus Petrus*, the brilliant but brief piece for two flutes and trumpet written to celebrate the seventieth birthday of Boulez. Nevertheless, within six months of completing the tuba work he had to produce another piece for soloist and orchestra, this time for the last night of the centenary season of the Proms. He had agreed with the BBC sometime earlier that the new work would be a concerto for the saxophonist John Harle. However, like his three earlier pieces for soloist and orchestra, *Panic* (95) is not a concerto in the traditional sense, but a work cast in a single span. He scored it for alto saxophone, drum kit and the wind and percussion sections of an orchestra. The inclusion of a drum kit player to be the soloist's sidekick conjures up memories of the brilliant alto saxophone playing of Charlie Parker and the new drum style of Kenny Clarke in the heyday of bebop. It may also conjure up memories of those incidents when Charlie Parker would contempuously turn his back on his audience when playing. Not that John Harle would ever do such a thing, yet there were many at the first performance who must have thought the the work Birtwistle had composed for him also showed contempt for the audience.

In many respects the contrasts with *The Cry of Anubis* are extreme. Although the work falls into three main sections, the structure within them is far from being clear cut. Tempos change irrationally, and as often as not the layering of the textures produces a density so opaque that it is almost impossible to disentangle them by ear. Among the few features *Panic* shares in common with the tuba piece are the easily recognizable repetitions and the constant return to the same note in certain passages. In one the saxophone has a series of ten expanding, arch-like phrases which always return to D♭, the instrument's lowest note.

Birtwistle claims that he composes for himself, not an audience. 'That's the only way I can hope to communicate with people,' he told me in 1983. 'Were I to think of an audience I'd probably think of the lowest common denominator, and I don't want that.' More recently he drew my attention to what Francis

Bacon had to say about working for an audience: 'What do you imagine an audience would want?' But if Birtwistle refuses to take the audience into account, he does respect the occasion for which a work is written. *The Cry of Anubis* was composed for an education concert for young people and its relative simplicity reflects this. His *Fanfare for Glyndebourne* (91) reflects not only what Glyndebourne is famous for but also that the Glyndebourne's touring company was to include an opera of his own in 1994. The fanfare represents him at his most dissonant and raucous, but it concludes with the tuba playing the opening of Mozart's Overture to *The Marriage of Figaro* in a key of the player's choice. The last night of the Proms is an occasion when everyone can let their hair down in the Albert Hall. But before the concluding high jinks the audience finds comfort in a cocoon of jingoism symbolized by the singing of 'Jerusalem' and 'Rule, Britannia'.

Birtwistle dedicated *Panic* to John Drummond, who had commissioned the work on behalf of the BBC. Under his dedication he heads the score:

> O what is he doing the great god Pan
> Down by the reeds by the river.
> Spreading ruin and scattering ban ...

adding 'something I remember from school but can't remember by whom. (A. Noyes maybe?)'

Had he gone to his bookshelves and extracted Palgrave's *Golden Treasury*, an anthology every grammar schoolboy like him had to have in the forties and fifties, he would have seen that the poet was Elizabeth Barrett Browning and that he had quoted (or rather misquoted) the opening lines of 'A Musical Instrument', her description of how Pan fashioned his pan-pipes.

> What was he doing, the great god Pan,
> Down in the reeds by the river?

Spreading ruin and scattering ban,
Splashing and paddling with hoofs of a goat,
And breaking the golden lilies afloat
With the dragon-fly on the river.

'The word Panic', says *Brewer's Dictionary of Phrase and Fable*, 'comes from the god Pan because the sounds heard at night in the mountains and valleys, which give rise to sudden and unwarranted fear, were attributed to him.' Panic is a feeling of terror which tends to affect a whole group of people, and to be in a state of panic means that those who experience it are plunged into utter confusion.

About a hundred million people heard *Panic* over radio and television when it was first performed, and judging from the letters the BBC received most people were outraged. It is probable that no other composer before Birtwistle has ever had so much abuse thrown at him by the popular press. Some people blamed the performance and the poor sound balance. When Decca produced a compact disc two years later of the same performers playing the work in a studio a few weeks after the first performance, it proved to be much less formidable. Textures were clearer, and there was no difficulty in relating the piece to what Birtwistle had been doing in the past.

The alto saxophone is a powerful, agile instrument with a range roughly equal to that of the clarinet. Normally it is only included in an orchestra to play expressive solos, its forceful tone being too dominant to blend successfully with a woodwind section when playing as an ensemble or chorus. Its relationship with an orchestra is therefore that of odd-man-out. So too is that of a drum kit. The precedent for basing a work on the conflict between a chorus and an odd-man-out who insists on going his own way is *Refrains and Choruses* (1) where the horn stands apart. In this, as in all the subsequent works based on this formula, the inevitable outcome of the conflict is a situation when the two parties cooperate with each other. In *Panic*, however, there is another issue at stake. This concerns the playing of expressive, legato solos, which would normally be the saxophone's prerogative as the soloist. But all the wind instruments involved with the work are potential soloists. Ideally, as in *The Cry of Anubis*, the best results would occur when soloist and orchestra share the task. In *Panic* this is not until the final section. Up until then, neither the soloist nor the orchestra is able to sustain a *cantus* line by itself without dissolving into stuttering repetitions.

The first of the work's three main sections exposes the conflict, the second takes the music to a shattering climax, the third moves towards reconciliation. The piece opens in a manner one would have expected from Birtwistle. As befits Elizabeth Barrett Browning's poem, the orchestra has swirling ostinatos to represent the river, while the saxophone gradually springs into activity by elaborating a reiterated E, quickly surging up to a high note, then switching to rapid figurations. So far the efforts of soloist and orchestra have been to coordinate. But when the saxophone begins a lyrical melody and attempts to coordinate with the orchestra's accompanying chords by reinforcing them with accents which destroy the smoothness of its line, the concord comes to an end. We have the first of the soloist's ineffectual repetitions, and thereafter he and his sidekick adopt tempos that are independent of the orchestra's. In the passages which follow all the efforts of the orchestra to establish a *cantus* come to nothing, and all the efforts of the soloist to dominate proceedings with its independent, highly elaborated line end in frustration and more ineffectual repetitions. It is, however, during the longest of these repetitive sections that the parties return to playing in the same tempo, and a measure of agreement is reattained.

The second main section begins slowly with the orchestra's woodwind unwinding a rich, legato texture. When the saxophone takes over from the first bassoon the balance is disturbed and once again the parties are thrown into conflict. The following episode is when the soloist plays the ten expanding, arch-like passages which return to D♭. In this episode its sidekick dictates the tempo that the trumpets and trombones should adopt in defiance of the conductor and the rest of the orchestra. After a while a new start is made, this time with the saxophone fitting neatly in with the arabesques the bass clarinet and bassoons are playing. Yet this too is short lived, for the soloist soon branches out on his own again. Eventually the conflict builds up to a massive climax. This turns out to be the peripeteia, for almost immediately afterwards the bass clarinet and bassoons begin a slow melody which it shares with the saxophone, each phrase beginning and ending on a D. However, the tessitura proves to be too low for the saxophone and before long it takes its own development of the line into a register more suitable for it. Thereafter the music is gradually transformed into a passage where the rapid ostinatos, which have been so prevalent throughout the work, come fully into their own. These prepare the ground for the triumphant conclusion to the work. Together the soloist and the high woodwind peal out a tune in unison, and to confirm the rapport between saxophone and orchestra, all those who can bring the piece to a conclusion by playing in unison D♭.

When the furore of its first performance has been forgotten, *Panic* will probably be thought of as a successor to *Tragoedia* (14), that is, as a work which reflects Birtwistle's belief that the ancient, pre-Socratic Greek world was as deeply sensuous as it was violent and raw, an era when actions and emotions were taken to extremes. In *Tragoedia* the trappings of tragedy are celebrated in terms of a raucous, turbulent goat dance. Even the central 'Stasimon' goes to an extreme, but to an opposite extreme – to that of absolute tranquillity. As far as Birtwistle is concerned there is little or no interest in Pan as the god of pastures or the fashioner of pan-pipes. This is only for someone who wants to idealize the Greek world. For him, Pan was a lewd, sensual being, with horns, snub nose and goat's feet, who found pleasure in frightening the wits out of people and 'spreading ruin'.

SLOW FRIEZE

Writing music in two or three tempos simultaneously need not create the utter confusion found in *Panic*. Both *Todtnauberg*, the Celan setting Birtwistle composed after the Prom piece, and *Slow Frieze*, the instrumental work which followed, involve the simultaneous presentation of independent tempos in ways few would find perplexing. (It was at this time that Birtwistle had the idea of writing a work for woodwind and brass instruments in which the tempo differences and fluctuations would have to be controlled by two conductors. Andrew Rosner, his agent, even obtained a joint commission for it from the London Sinfonietta and the Los Angeles Philharmonic. It was to have been ready for the Sinfonietta's thirtieth anniversary in 1998. But when he had the time to write it after the completion of *Exody*, Birtwistle's enthusiasm had waned, and he postponed it until his 'juices' were stimulated again.)

Slow Frieze (97) was written for Joanna MacGregor and thirteen members of the London Sinfonietta – four woodwind, three brass, a percussionist playing untuned percussion instruments, and five strings. The piece draws together and develops ideas he had introduced in *An Interrupted Endless Melody, Antiphonies, Five Distances* and *Panic*. As in *Five Distances* the groups are spatially separated. Brass and strings are placed on either side of the pianist, who as the soloist occupies the central position, while the woodwind and percussionist sit as far back as possible. For the most part the woodwind play the *cantus*, their entries being cued by the percussionist; the remaining instrumentalists, including the pianist, function as the *continuum* and play under the direction of a conductor.

In that the *cantus* is largely independent of the rhythmically orientated *continuum*, the work is not unlike *An Interrupted Endless Melody*. There the oboe player had the freedom to choose between two different versions of the melody, to decide whether to go on or to go back when a certain sign is reached and to employ different dynamics. In *Slow Frieze* each woodwind instrument has two melodies or modes as Birtwistle calls them, and has the freedom to choose how the various versions of the 'modes' can be realized in performance.

As in the oboe piece, those who accompany the *cantus* are controlled. Following what he had done in *Antiphonies*, Birtwistle once again treats the piano as a tuned percussion instrument. Although he provides it with music suitable for a virtuoso and has it dominate most of the work's nineteen short sections, its rhythmically focused ostinatos are never likely to detract the listener from the floating melodies given to the woodwind. Most of the music for the strings and brass is also in the form of ostinatos. Many are varied in Birtwistle's usual manner, but some of them are simply literal repetitions similar to those found in *Panic*. Indeed no other Birtwistle piece contains so many types of ostinato. The work also offers a good example of the way he interlocks different patterns to create a sense of discontinuity. One very noticeable pattern is built from a cluster of semitones moving in demisemiquavers at a rate of quaver = 168. It first occurs on the trumpet. About a minute later it reappears quite out of the blue on violins and viola. Later and equally unexpectedly it comes back in a varied form on the viola. Still later appearances occur on the first violin and then the viola again. If all these incidences were placed in sequence we would have a perfectly logical continuity. One thing would lead to another. But since we hear only sections of the overall pattern interspersed with other types of material, the logic of the continuity is destroyed. One event does not necessarily lead to another. That said, however, one has to admit that the piece does hang together in some mysterious way. Perhaps listeners supply the continuity for themselves. In fact, this is a situation Birtwistle has relied on throughout his career, and is why his discontinuities actually appear to make sense.

PULSE SHADOWS

William Empson provided the most vivid illustration of the poetic potential of discontinuities in his *Seven Types of Ambiguity*.* To make his point, he took one of the poems Arthur Waley had translated from the Chinese:

> Swiftly the years, beyond recall,
> Solemn the stillness of this spring morning.

'Lacking rhyme, metre, and any overt device such as comparison,' wrote Empson, 'these lines are what we should normally call poetry only by virtue of their compactness; two statements are made as if they were connected, and the reader is forced to consider their relationship for himself. The reason why these facts should have been selected for a poem is left for him to invent; he will invent a variety of reasons and order them in his own mind. This, I think, is the essential fact about the poetic use of language.'

It could be said that this applies to everything Birtwistle has written. It is particularly relevant to *Pulse Shadows* (101) which alternates his *Nine Movements for String Quartet* (100) with his *Nine Settings of Celan* (99). He calls them 'two parallel sequences of music representing two "streams of consciousness", one being a comment on the other, or alternatively one being the other's alter ego'. However he leaves it to listeners to discover the relationship between them. His model is Boulez's *Le Marteau sans maître*, which has been a direct influence on his way of thinking ever since he first heard it in the fifties. Boulez sets three poems: *Bourreaux de solitude* has three instrumental commentaries, *L'Artisanat furieux* an instrumental prelude and postlude, *Bel édifice et les pressentiments* a 'double'. Since all three have other versions of themselves, the work includes three logical

* William Empson, *Seven Types of Ambiguity*, Chatto and Windus, London 1930. Third, revised, edition 1953, pp. 23–5.

sequences. But Boulez breaks them up and places them in an order that disguises the fact.

'L'Artisanat' Cycle	'Bourreaux' Cycle	'Bel Edifice' Cycle
1 Avant 'L'Artisanat'		
2	Commentaire I	
3 'L'Artisanat furieux'		
4	Commentaire II	
5		'Bel édifice'
6	'Bourreaux de solitude'	
7 Après 'L'Artisanat'		
8	Commentaire III	
9		'Bel édifice' double

The first example of Birtwistle's adoption of this procedure occurs in *Monody for Corpus Christi* (2) where two songs are separated by an instrumental movement 'quasi fanara'. The import of the first song (a vision of Christ as a dead knight) comes after that of the last (a lullaby to the infant Jesus) so that listeners are bound to interpret the sequence as representing death and rebirth. However, they will have to decide for themselves the significance of the fanfare. Later, when he came to compose *Entr'actes and Sappho Fragments* (11), the sequence of events became more ambiguous. The work began life as a set of five entr'actes composed to go with Debussy's Sonata for flute, viola and harp. Then quite independently he wrote five settings of poems by Sappho for soprano and an ensemble which included oboe, violin and percussion as well as those used for the entr'actes. Finally he interspersed new versions of the entr'actes between the songs. At one time he used to say that something strange happens to the entr'actes in the new context – 'A chemical change takes place.' Now he claims that the new versions are also commentaries on the songs. They offer a different perspective on what is being sung.

In *Cantata* (28), five instrumental refrains are interspersed among settings of tombstone inscriptions, other lines from Sappho and quotations from *The Greek Anthology*. In my first book I interpreted the fluctuating nature of these refrains as being commentaries on the fragmentary texts which have no obvious connection and resemble the discontinuities found in inner speech. But I admit that this was only my opinion. Given the nature of the piece, others will be bound to interpret it differently.

The song sets that followed in the eighties lack instrumental movements, but Birtwistle included them in *Four Poems by Jaan Kaplinski* (82) where they focus on rhythmic development as opposed to the melodic development in the songs. As mentioned above, he maintains that this was when *Pulse Shadows* first came into his mind. The fact that it would ultimately contain nine songs and nine quartet movements may have also been influenced by the division of *Le marteau sans maître* into nine movements.

Although anguish, darkness and the shadow of death are present in all Celan's poems, those that Birtwistle chose to set nevertheless contain hope and a sense of optimism. As often as not these positive aspirations are symbolized by the approach of light. *With Letter and Clock*, the poem he selected to set for his inauguration as Henry Purcell Professor of Composition at King's College, has as its refrain 'Swimming light, will you come now?' The word 'light' is also prominent in the first and last songs in the cycle. The first, *Thread suns*, begins with an image of a 'grey-black wilderness', but when a tree-high thought 'tunes into light's pitch' the poet can say that 'there are still songs to be sung on the other side of mankind'. In the last song, *Give the Word*, the word light is reserved for the very end. Birtwistle asks for the high A♭ on which it appears to be amplified, given a degree of reverberation and to swell to quadruple forte so that the sound note bearing the word fills the concert hall.

In this context even those songs in which the word light is absent, such as *Tenebrae* and *Night*, become more positive than when they appeared in the *Three Settings of Celan* of 1992.

The cry 'We are near, Lord' becomes one of keen anticipation. The vision of 'the red of two mouths' appearing 'like stars' in the 'cosmic network of rails' becomes more vividly 'conceivable'. 'Psalm' reads like a devotional song addressed to a god who has deserted the speaker or has ceased to exist: 'No one moulds us again out of earth and clay, / no one conjures our dust. / No one.' Birtwistle treats this as a cry from the heart, yet he immediately responds in his setting to the sudden switch from accusation to praise and acknowledgement. He confirms that the absent god has to be found: 'Praised be your name, no one. / For your sake / we shall flower. / Towards / you.' Even 'An Eye, open', ostensibly one of the grimmest poems in the cycle, conjures up the prospect of 'hours, May-coloured, cool'.

As in most if not all of his works, Birtwistle also wanted to focus on reconciliation. This is undoubtedly why he chose to set *Todtnauberg*, a poem in which Celan had hoped to find reconciliation with someone who had openly backed the Nazis. Todtnauberg was the Black Forest retreat of Martin Heidegger, which Celan visited in 1967 on the invitation of the philosopher. Each man admired the other's work, but whereas Celan had suffered at the hands of the Nazis, Heidegger had been one of their keenest supporters. Since the war he had chosen to remain silent about his commitment to them. Celan hoped his poem might break the silence, and that the two men could be open about what happened under Hitler. Birtwistle prefaces his score with the words Celan wrote in Heidegger's guest book: 'Into the hut-book, looking at the well-star with a hope for a caring word in the heart'. To embody the spirit of reconciliation he has the soprano both sing the text and speak it in rapid alternation. If the language of the sung version is German then that of the spoken version should be English, or vice versa. As mentioned when discussing *Slow Frieze*, the song involves the simultaneous presentation of different tempos. The spoken version should be delivered at a tempo of quaver = 60/84 'in a light, precise, factual manner'. The sung version, along with the clarinets who shadow it, shifts rapidly from quaver = 56 to quaver = 60 or quaver = 84. The strings, on the other hand, cut across both versions by playing permutations of irregular patterns of beats interspersed by repetitions of a short refrain at a tempo of semiquaver = 204. On paper this seems complicated, but in performance the differing tempos clarify the texture. One interesting point is that Birtwistle wants the spoken text to sound hesitant as if to suggest that reconciliation had only been broached and there was still an element of doubt in Celan's mind.

In the published edition of *Nine Movements for String Quartet*, the items are simply referred to as movements and are placed roughly in the order of composition. In *Pulse Shadows*, however, they are divided into four *Friezes* and five *Fantasias*, and placed in a different order. As I mentioned when discussing the set of three assembled in 1993, the Friezes (other than the first) remain in the same tempo and metre, and develop rhythmical figures without changing their basic characters. The Fantasias fluctuate in tempo and metre, and change completely the character of the rhythmical figures they use. The latter are the more volatile, and this is why Birtwistle chose to begin *Pulse Shadows* with one that immediately catches the attention with its vigour and transforms its basic figure in a way that allows the quiet opening of *Thread Suns* to creep in almost unnoticed. In fact Birtwistle has the quartet quietly repeat over and over again the end of the Fantasia for about half the length of the song in order to suggest that there might be a connection between the instrumental and vocal items.

The order of the items in the complete work is as follows:

Quartet Cycle	Celan Cycle
1 Fantasia 1	
2	'Thread Suns'
3 Frieze 1	
4	'White and Light'
5 Fantasia 2	
6	'Psalm'

Quartet Cycle	Celan Cycle
7 Fantasia 3	
8	'With Letter and Clock'
9 Frieze 2	
10	'An Eye, open'
11 Fantasia 4	
12	'Todtnauberg'
13 Frieze 3	
14	'Tenebrae'
15 Fantasia 5	
16	'Night'
17 Frieze 4 – Todesfuge	
18	'Give the Word'

Todesfuge is Celan's most famous and widely anthologized poem. Birtwistle considered it unsuitable for a song because it concerns Jewish prisoners being tyrannized by a camp commandant and is too direct and realistic for anything other than an abstract setting. What he admires in particular about Celan's poetry is that it exists on several layers. He has therefore no need to focus on one particular musical image. His music can be as ambiguous as the verse. However the meaning of *Todesfuge* is too obvious to allow for this. On the grounds that in at least one concentration camp the commandant had Jewish fiddlers play a well-known tango whenever torture, grave digging and executions took place, Celan originally called the poem *Tango of Death*. He changed it to *Fugue of Death* because fugues represent the art of music at its most elevated, and Bach fugues could be heard coming from the commandant's residence at Auschwitz as prisoners were marched to the gas chambers. Yet it was not the contrast between the elevated and the grotesque that interested Birtwistle, it was that being a *Frieze* his fugue could present the three highly character-ized rhythmic figures designed for the subject and counter-subject in a way that preserved their vigour and character right through to the end. The resultant energy and determination is reminiscent of Beethoven's *Grosse Fuge*. Moreover, in the context of Celan's poems, it seems to epitomize, like Beethoven's fugue, the will to overcome adversity. Remnants of one of its rhythmic patterns continue to linger on through the whole of the last song so that the word 'light' appears to be the inevitable outcome of its striving.

Birtwistle says that the cycle of songs can be performed independently of the cycle of quartets and indeed the order can be changed or only a few need be given if the singer so wishes. The same applies to the quartets. But when the two cycles are combined to form *Pulse Shadows*, I think the order selected for the published score and the first performances in Witten and London in April 1996 is the most satifactory, and I believe that Birtwistle shares this opinion. He maintains that he never intended the quartets to have a direct bearing on the songs or the songs on the quartets, but perhaps, like me, he has now established connections between them, and convinced himself that the relationships are demonstrable. This may be speculation, yet one thing is absolutely sure: *Pulse Shadows* will eventually be considered one of the finest, most moving works of the century.

4

The Composer in Conversation

The following is a résumé of conversations held in Mere, Wiltshire on 6 November 1997, when we had the proofs of Exody 23: 59: 59: *on the table in front of us, and later on 8 December when he had just completed the first of his piano pieces,* Harrison's Clocks.

EXODY 23: 59: 59

When I was here a year ago you were calling Exody 'Maze'. *Why the change?*

Simply because I wanted something more ambiguous. At first I thought of 'sequences'. Then I heard an interview the Canadian poet, Robin Blaser, gave on Radio 3's *Night Waves* last January. I liked what he said so I sent away for a volume of his poems. He'd chosen the word 'exody' to be the title of a group of six which ended the book. It has the same meaning as 'exodus', but its use is rare.* Since he had no objection to my borrowing it, I adopted *Sequences for 23:59:59* for my subtitle. Subsequently I dropped the word 'sequences' altogether. The numbers of course refer to the last moment of the day or the year, the century or the millennium. All last moments are oxymoronic. They're an end and a beginning. The last second before the end of this millennium will be the moment when we'll be greeting the next millennium. An exody may be a departure, but it is also an arrival.

* In the 1971 edition of the *Oxford English Dictionary* there is only one illustration of its use. It comes from a novel by George MacDonald dating from 1882: 'The plomp of the cork's exody, and the gurgle of the wine . . . speedily consoled him'.

Did the change of title mean a change of structure?

No, the piece is still about journeying through a maze, a journey that ends at the place where it started from. There are interruptions from time to time, but it's cast in one long continuous line – one huge linear progression from beginning to end. The line itself is very like a piece of wool or thread. It consists of various strands woven together to make one. At certain times it can be unwound so that the strands can be seen, and when you look closer you can see that they're made up from finer strands twisted together. In fact there are an infinite numbers of ways it can be divided up. [He points to pages 75–77 of the full score where the line is divided into eleven parts, and then to page 83 where only a flute is playing it.] Sometimes I want certain features of the line to be illuminated. This is why I include parts for two saxophones. They're not normally found in an orchestra so they stand out. I'm particularly interested in their vocal qualities. When they play, the line is at its most lyrical. To give them additional prominence, I have them play in different tempos from each other as well as that of the orchestra when they first come in.

Is this the only time you use independent tempos in the work?

Yes. In this respect the piece is quite different from *Five Distances*, *Panic* or *Slow Frieze*. Apart from this instance there are no other places where instruments branch out into independent tempos. What I have done, however, is coordinate the tempos throughout the piece. To do this I devised a 'pulse shuttle'.

So that to ply between 48 and 160 you can either go via 64–96–128 or 72–96–120. I take it that 96 functions as a junction, and when you reach it you can change routes.

And the ratios between the tempos are very simple. It's just a question of multiplying or dividing by two or three. By this method I've produced tempos that are not included on the

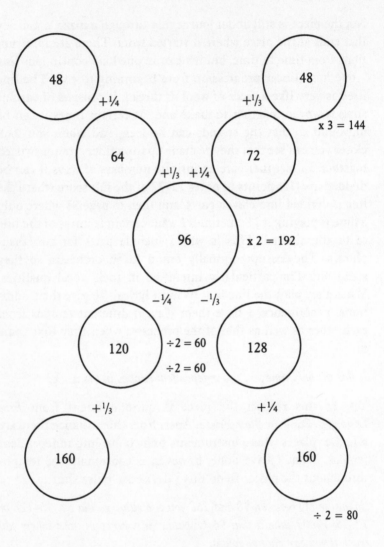

The diagram of the pulse shuttle

shuttle. The alto sax's 144 when it first comes in is three times as fast as the orchestra's 48, the soprano sax's 128 is a third faster than 96, which in turn is twice as fast as the orchestra's 48.

What about your journey through the labyrinth? It would be totally unlike you if you didn't have to retrace you steps or take another path when you found yourself back to where you'd been before.

The journey is the line running through the piece. Like Paul Klee, I'm 'taking a line for a walk'.* But the lines Klee draws are pure continuum, they look like a map of a walk or a journey. And this is how we usually think of journeys – fluid things which are uninterrupted. But when you're in the process of journeying, you perceive them differently. You don't look straight ahead, you look to the right and then to the left. And when you turn to the left you fail to take in the events on the right and vice-versa. In retrospect you think of the journey as being a logical progression from one thing to another, but in actual fact it consists of a series of unrelated things, which means that you're simply making choices all the time, choices about where to look. It's to do with discontinuity. You have a continuum, but you're cutting things out of it while you look the other way.

The line I take for a walk in *Exody* does return to places I've been to before. This G, for instance. [He points to the long G that begins in bar 479 on page 82.] That relates to the long G that occurs near the beginning of the piece [bar 15]. I call its reappearance a 'gateway'. It comes after a huge down beat, and I've drawn attention to it with a distinctive rhythmic gesture on the bass drum. In this respect it's not unlike the function of the bass drum in *Ritual Fragment*. There are other gateways too, though this is the most important. There's one that occurs when a high E is reached. Gateways are like cuts, they open up another way of proceeding. They take you back to a previous stage on the

* Paul Klee, *Pedagogical Sketchbook*, Faber and Faber, London 1968, p. 16 – 'An active line on a walk, moving freely, without goal. A walk for a walk's sake.'

journey. On this occasion I return to the original G but look to the right rather than the left, or the left rather than the right when I go through the music again. In other words, you see those things that were missing the first time round.

You did something like that thirty years ago in Three Lessons in a Frame. *The first two lessons, if I remember correctly, are for piano alone and instruments alone, but what they actually play is the same work twice. Whatever is implied but missing in one version is to be found in the other.*

Yes, it's basically the same principle.

When I was here last year you showed me a chart which enabled you to see at a glance what notes you needed to create symmetry. Did you continue to use it?

I had it fixed to the wall above my desk, but took it down when I got to about halfway through the work because I lost interest in it. The journey I was embarking on was both musical and personal, but there's a difference between a journey that's prescribed and one on which you can take paths that catch your attention. On the musical level, an idea that has not been prescribed is more potent than one which has. Nevertheless I sometimes find that it's very useful to have something prescribed. I made great use of those symmetries, and I made other pre-compositional plans for certain sections of the work as well.

But I've been saying throughout this book that you abandoned these when you were writing Yan Tan Tethera. *What about 'the sanctity of the context'?*

That's still paramount. All I'm saying is that I find preordained ideas useful from time to time. The chart was intended to relate areas of pitch, and it was also to do with the line and things being placed upon it. One of its functions was to avoid the line and the windows becoming synchronized. Windows are short passages of ostinatos superimposed on the line to give you glimpses of something that might be happening beyond it.

The symmetries the chart helped me to see at a glance start here. [Bar 121 on page 27.] All the chords and textures from there until bar 249 on page 52 are symmetrical. It's after then that the windows begin to occur.

I know that there are one or two absolutely symmetrical chords to be found in your music, but I thought that usually you tried to avoid absolute symmetry because it created harmonic stasis.

That's true, but in this particular instance I want the harmony to be static. I want surface movement and inner stillness to be present at one and the same time. The opening is also very still. As you point out in this book, I've been interested in the relationship between movement and stillness for quite some time now.

And to get out of the maze you presumably have to return to those extremely widely spaced Cs that begin the piece.

Those Cs end my piano concerto [*Antiphonies*], my last concert piece involving a symphony orchestra, and they come back at the end of this one. At the beginning they're held for three bars, and then in bar 4 the violins and glockenspiel move up to D so that D becomes the highest note. The G that emerges shortly afterwards is the axis of symmetry between the high D and the low C. But at the end of the work in order to return to where I began I have to move down from G to F♯, the note that is equidistant between the two Cs. There it is on the three trombones [He points to bars 681–2]. Gradually the F♯ become more pervasive until eventually it resolves down to an E.

Yes, but at that point the Cs are no longer sounding. All you have during the last two bars is the E. To my ear it sounds like a typically modal resolution.

Yes, but as you've also pointed out in this book, the essence of my harmony is the tension between symmetrically based procedures and those based on modes. I don't know why I had to end on an E, it just had to be. My ear dictated it.

HARRISON'S CLOCKS

These are fiendishly difficult pieces I'm writing for Joanna MacGregor. (Although when I showed her the first one, she hardly batted an eyelid.) Each consists of a series of musical mechanisms which are meant to be as intricate as those found in a beautifully constructed clock. In this first one I wind the piece down in a manner that's supposed to resemble clockwork winding down. I've made use of this kind of ending on a number of occasions. *Five Distances* is a good example. The piece has to be played as fast as possible, and like most of the Friezes in *Nine Movements for String Quartet*, which it strongly resembles, remains in the same metre throughout. It begins with the right hand establishing a rhythmic ostinato mainly in triplets. Then the left hand comes in with another rhythmic ostinato, this one in duplets. The one responds to the other sometimes with something similar, at other times with something completely different. The general idea is that when one hand changes its pattern the other remains constant so that the two patterns nearly always overlap. As might be expected the piece involves repetitions, but because they're varied the music's in a constant state of development – rhythmic development – and in this sense it directly contrasts with *Exody*, which is in a constant state of melodic development. I got the idea from reading Dava Sobel's *Longitude*,* the story of how the eighteenth-century clock maker, John Harrison, solved the problem of measuring longitude. Until then sailors lost their bearings as soon as they lost sight of land. In England the situation reached a crisis in 1707 when a fleet of naval vessels carrying two thousand men perished off the Scilly Islands through faulty navigation. A prize was offered by the

---

* Dava Sobel, *Longitude*, Fourth Estate, London 1996.

government to solve 'the longitude problem', and Harrison eventually won it. He spent forty years inventing four clocks which could keep precise time at sea. For various reasons this had been impossible before, and without knowing how the time in Greenwich or another place of known longitude differed from the time on board ship longitude could not be measured. On board a ship clocks had to be altered each day to coincide with the sun at its zenith. All four are now in the Maritime Museum. Well, because of the name Harrison, and because they were highly intricate mechanisms, these clocks got my juices going.

What's the fascination with mechanisms? They crop up over and over again in your music.

It's the idea of ostinato – also the fascination with something that's secondary in music. Ostinatos are mechanisms, but have usually been used only for accompaniments. In *Secret Theatre*, and indeed in a great many works before that, I brought them into the foreground. I'm interested in the idea of using ostinato to make rhythmic pieces without any melodic content.

I suppose the models are those Bach Toccatas where harmony and rhythm predominate and melody is reduced to a minimum. My second piece for Joanna will be a toccata involving extremely rapid alternation of the hands. But ostinatos are not the only things I've wanted to raise from a secondary status to a primary one. I did the same with those entr'actes in *Entr'actes and Sappho Fragments*. No one takes much notice of the entr'actes when they go to the theatre. Mine are fragments, little moments of music, but when I wrote new versions of them and placed these between the songs they are not just interludes to relax the tension between the main items, they're pieces that have bearing on what is being sung. They have the same status as the instrumental movements in *Le marteau sans maître* have. If the accompanying instrumental parts are making a commentary on the texts when the songs are being sung, the instrumental movements extend the commentary beyond the time when the singer is singing.

I gather that when you've finished these piano pieces you're going to write two theatre works. Last year we talked about one that Covent Garden had commissioned for 2000.

THE LAST SUPPER

That's been postponed until the following year. For 2000 I'm writing a work for Glyndebourne Touring Opera to celebrate the millennium, and I've decided it'll be about the Last Supper.

Can you really make an opera of that?

Certainly – thirteen blokes sitting round a table is rather intriguing, don't you think! I also have a protagonist and a chorus. I'm really interested in the idea of the form of it – a dramatic tableau. Also the idea of the ritual which they go through. It's a ritual that's being invented, because when he says to them 'Drink this in remembrance of me' it's never been done before. He's telling them what they have to do. It's the initiation of something completely new. It's a beginning – an ending and a beginning. There are loads of musical and formal possibilities. It'll last about an hour and a quarter, I think. And I'd like the first performance to be in Durham Cathedral. I might also compose a mass to be sung in the background.

Do you remember when Francis Bacon was asked why he painted the crucifixion he talked about the lack of big subjects. When you deal with a big subject like the crucifixion it's already giving you so much. That's exactly what I feel about the Last Supper. And as far as I know nobody has tackled it before. I've asked Robin Blaser to write the libretto and I'm waiting to see what he comes up with.

THE MINOTAUR

Last year you told me you were going to base your Covent Garden opera on Stanislav Lem's science fiction novel Solaris. *After reading it I real-*

ized it would be ideal for you because it's the Orpheus legend in a new guise and it's also about being taken over by memories. The story hinges on the notion that the planet's ocean is a huge brain that turns memo-. ries of people into flesh and blood.

Yes, it would have been ideal, but we ran into copyright difficulties and then discovered that someone else had made an opera out of it. To replace it I have a script by Friedrich Dürrenmatt about the Minotaur that Minos kept in his labyrinth. It's the last thing Dürrenmatt wrote, I believe, and it's actually a scenario for a ballet. His widow gave me the script when I was in Basle for a performance of *Silbury Air*, and it was she who suggested that I might be interested in making an opera out of it. I looked at it and realized that it could be formally related to *The Mask of Orpheus*, that's to say I could carry the narrative forward by means of either dancing or singing.

The following is a précis of the story as told by Dürrenmatt:
The Minotaur is a monstrous creature with the head of a bull and the body of a man. The action takes place in the labyrinth built to protect human beings from the Minotaur and the Minotaur from human beings. The walls are made from reflecting glass. The first part deals with the dance the creature has with the countless reflections of himself. For him they are not reflections but creatures that resemble him. A girl enters the labyrinth, and when he begins to dance, she begins to dance. 'He danced his monstrosity, she danced her beauty, he danced his joy at finding her, she danced her fear at having been found by him, he danced his salvation, she danced her fate . . . They danced, and their reflections danced, and he did not know that he took the girl, nor could he know that he killed her, since he did not know what life and death were.' A flock of birds flies into the labyrinth, and as he looks up to watch them flying away, the sun burns an image into his brain, an image of a mighty turning wheel, 'the wheel of the curse that weighed on him. the wheel of his fate, the wheel of his birth and the wheel of his death.' A man comes into the labyrinth, a man with a sword. The Minotaur approaches him in good will, but the man lunges at him and wounds him. Six girls and six

*other youths appear before him holding hands, and the Minotaur feels
that 'all of humanity is closing in on him to destroy him'. His eyes fill
with rage. He attacks them, 'tearing out limbs, guzzling blood, breaking
bones, rummaging in bellies and wombs'. He becomes aware that the
creatures he has been dancing with since being in the labyrinth are his
reflections. 'And gradually it dawned on him that he was facing
himself.'*

*While he sleeps, Ariadne attaches a red thread around his horns. On
awakening, he sees a creature that looks like himself, but is clearly not
his reflection. It is Theseus dressed like the Minotaur. 'When the
Minotaur rushed into the other's arms, confident of having found a
friend, a creature like himself . . . the other struck . . . and so surely did
the other sink his dagger into the Minotaur's back that he was already
dead when he sank to the ground.'*

It's the awakening of self-consciousness, a condition only obtainable by human beings, which the Minotaur is not. It's also a
myth that everyone knows. There's nothing worse than using
something nobody knows. It belongs to the same category of
myth as Orpheus. In that sense it's a suitable case for treatment.
There's the labyrinth (which relates it to *Exody*), and there are
also mirrors. The mirrors could function like screens and allow a
dancer to take over from a singer or vice-versa. The whole piece
is a series of duets – somebody confronting the bull: the girl, the
man with the sword, his companions, Theseus. (There is also the
episode with the birds.) The sequence is: the bull alone – the
entrance of second person or a group of people – confrontation –
duet – a death or a series of deaths – the bull alone (or at the end
Theseus alone). Moving between text and dance must be done in
a properly constructed way. You might get the bull talking to the
dancer who could only answer in action, mime or dance. Or you
might get singer bull and singer Theseus singing a duet, or any
combination of these things. The labyrinthine aspect of the piece
is reflected in the way these two means of expression alternate.
And because you're doing things by means of mirrors, you could

make the second act a mirror of the first, a different representation of the same story. The second version could develop different aspects of the story – aspects you didn't do the first time round. The first act could focus on the inner world, the second on the outer world and the pagan environment.

It seemed to be a genuine extension of the Orpheus idea. But, of course, you can't repeat Orpheus. It'll be very different from Orpheus and yet belong to a similar type of theatricality. You could have a cycle of time by means of a mechanical sun. The first act could take place in daylight, the second at night. I've asked David Harsent to write the libretto, but since he can't get started until 1999, I'm not going to have much time to write the score.

But meanwhile let me give you another quote with which you can end your book if you want. It comes from a book by the American painter Philip Guston, but since I've lent it to somebody I can't give you a reference. It may not be as succinct as the one you used in the first paragraph of your introductory chapter, yet I think it's an even better description of what I'm trying to do.

To will a new form is unacceptable, because will builds distortions. Desire, too, is incomplete and arbitrary. These strategies, however intricate they become, must expressibly be removed to clear the way for something else – a situation somewhat unclear, but which is a very precise act.

Catalogue of Works

1. *Refrains and Choruses* for wind quintet (flute, oboe, clarinet, horn and bassoon). Duration 8 minutes.
In seven sections: through repetition, the refrain (the recurring element) becomes a predominant entity and so the chorus (the constant element) of the following section.
Completed New Year's Eve, 1957. Dedicated to Alexander Goehr.
First performed at 1959 Cheltenham Festival by Portia Wind Ensemble, Town Hall, Cheltenham, 11 July 1959.
Recorded 1) by Danzi Wind Quintet (1966) on Philips SAL 3669. U.E. 12931.
2) Netherlands Wind Ensemble (1991) on Etcetera KCT 1130.

2. *Monody for Corpus Christi* for soprano, flute, horn and violin. Duration 12 minutes.
Text: the old English carol, 'The Faucon hath borne my make away', and James, John and Robert Wedderburn's lullaby, 'O my deare hert young Jesu sweit.'
Composed 1959. Dedicated to Alan Lambert.
First performed by Dorothy Dorow and the New Music Ensemble, conducted by John Carewe, Recital Room, Royal Festival Hall, 5 April 1960
U.E. 12928.

3. *Three Sonatas for Nine Instruments*. Scheduled for performance by New Music Ensemble, conducted by John Carewe, at 1960 Aldeburgh Festival, Jubilee Hall, 17 June 1960; withdrawn after first rehearsal.
Unpublished.

4. *Précis* for piano solo. Duration 4 minutes.
Composed summer 1960. Dedicated to John Ogdon.
First performed by John Ogdon at Dartington Summer School of Music, Dartington Hall, August 1960.
Recorded (1965) by John Ogdon on HMV ALP 2098 or ASD 645. (LP deleted)
U.E. 14158.
(Printed score – and recording – inaccurate; Maxwell Davies owns the corrected copy.)

5. *The World is Discovered.* Six instrumental movements after Heinrich Isaac (1450–1517) for two flutes, oboe, cor anglais, two clarinets (second doubling basset horn or bass clarinet), two horns, two bassoons, harp and guitar. Duration 12 minutes.
Three verses with three choruses; amplifies facets of *Der Weld fundt, Tmeiskin uas iunch, Helogierons nous, Et ie boi d'autant* and *Maudit soi* (Denkmäler der Tonkunst in Österreich, Jahrg. XIV/I, band 28).
Commissioned by Tonus Musical Promotions (Anthony Friese-Green). Completed January 1961. Dedicated to Peter Maxwell Davies.
First performed by Portia Wind Ensemble (with Marie Goossens and John Williams), conducted by James Verity, Recital Room, Royal Festival Hall, 6 March 1961.
U.E. 12937.

6. *Entr'actes* for flute, viola and harp. Duration *c.* 15 minutes.
A cycle of five movements with coda: later the first part of *Entr'actes and Sappho Fragments* (11).
Completed July 1962.
First performed by members of the Bournemouth Symphony Orchestra, Cranborne Chase School, Wardour Castle, autumn 1962.
Not published separately.

7. *Chorales for Orchestra* for 3 flutes (all doubling piccolos), 3 oboes (3rd doubling cor anglais), 3 clarinets (2nd doubling E♭ clarinet, 3rd doubling bass clarinet), 3 bassoons (3rd doubling contra), 4 horns, 4 trumpets, 3 trombones, tuba, 2 harps, percussion (6 players) and strings. Duration 20 minutes.
Composed between December 1960 and October 1963.
First performed by New Philharmonia Orchestra, conducted by Edward Downes, Royal Festival Hall, 14 February 1967.
U.E. 12955.

8. *Narration: A Description of the Passing of a Year* for a cappella chorus. Duration 11 minutes.
Text: sections 22 and 23 of the fourteenth-century romance, *Sir Gawain and the Green Knight*, translated by Brian Stone (Penguin Classics, 1959).
Composed October and November 1963.
First performed by John Alldis Choir, conducted by John Alldis, Wigmore Hall, 14 February 1964.
U.E. 14157.

9. *Music for Sleep* for children's voices, piano and percussion (at least three players). A lullaby for children under 11 to perform. Duration 15 minutes.
Commissioned by *Musical Times* and *Music in Education* (Novello and Co. Ltd) and published in their editions of March 1964. Composed November 1963. Dedicated 'To the boys and girls of my two schools: Knighton House and Port Regis.'
First performed by pupils of Knighton House and Port Regis Schools under the direction of the composer, Bryanston School, winter 1963.

10. *Three Movements with Fanfares* for chamber orchestra – flute (doubling piccolo), oboe, clarinet, bassoon, 2 horns, 2 trumpets, 2 trombones, harp, timps (doubling percussion), strings. Duration 14 minutes.

Commissioned by the Worshipful Company of Musicians for the 1964 City of London Festival.
First performed by English Chamber Orchestra, conducted by John Pritchard, Guildhall, 8 July 1964.
U.E. 12989.

11. *Entr'actes and Sappho Fragments* for soprano, flute, oboe, violin, viola, harp and percussion. Duration 25 minutes.
Texts taken from *The Greek Anthology, with an English translation*, Harvard University Press, 1916–18.
Five entr'actes with coda, a connecting movement in which voice sings wordlessly, then five songs interspersed with new version of the entr'actes and a second coda.
Completed spring 1964.
First performed at 1964 Cheltenham Festival by Mary Thomas and Virtuoso Ensemble of London, conducted by John Carewe, Town Hall, Cheltenham, 11 July 1964.
U.E. 12948.

12. *Ring a Dumb Carillon* for soprano (doubling suspended cymbals), clarinet and percussion. Duration 12 minutes.
Text: Christopher Logue's 'On a matter of prophecy' from *Wand and Quadrant*, Collection Merlin (Olympia Press, 1953).
A dramatic scena in which the clarinet carries the monody.
Composed winter 1964–5.
First performed by Noelle Barker, Alan Hacker and Christopher Seaman at an ICA concert, Arts Council, London, 19 March 1965.
Recorded by Mary Thomas, Alan Hacker and Barry Quinn on Mainstream MS 5001, LP deleted.
U.E. 14192.

13. *Carmen Paschale* Motet for SATB with organ obbligato. Duration 6 minutes.
Text (in Latin) by Sedulus Scottus (*c.* 850) in Helen Waddell's

Mediaeval Latin Lyrics, Constable, 1929.
Commissioned by BBC Transcription Service for 1965 Aldeburgh Festival. Completed New Year's Day, 1965.
First performed by Purcell Singers, conducted by Imogen Holst, with Simon Preston, Aldeburgh Parish Church, 17 June 1965.
U.E. 12975.

14. *Tragoedia* for flute, oboe, clarinet, horn and bassoon (all doubling claves), two violins, viola, cello and harp. Duration 15 minutes.
Based on the formal structures of Greek tragedy: Prologue – Parados – Episodion (Strophe, Anapaest, Antistrophe) – Stasimon – Episodion – Exodos.
Commissioned by the Melos Ensemble. Composed spring 1965. Dedicated to Michael Tippett on his 60th birthday.
First performed by Melos Ensemble, conducted by Lawrence Foster, Wardour Castle Summer School of Music, 20 August 1965.
Recorded by 1) Melos Ensemble, conducted by Lawrence Foster on HMV ASD 2333, reissued on Argo ZRG 750 (LP deleted);
2) Ensemble InterContemporain, conducted by Pierre Boulez, on Deutsche Grammophon 439 910–2.
U.E. 14179.

15. *Verses* for clarinet and piano. Duration 6 minutes.
Composed autumn 1965. Dedicated to Alan Hacker.
First performed by Alan Hacker and Stephen Prusling, Architectural Association, Bedford Square, London, October 1965.
U.E. 14206.

16. *The Mark of the Goat* Dramatic cantata from actors, singers, two choruses, three melody instruments, three players at one piano, large and small percussion ensemble. Duration 35 minutes.

Text by Alan Crang.

The action (in four scenes) involves the defiance of a military dictator by women anxious to give decent burial to a political martyr. Suitable for children between the ages of eleven and thirteen.

Commissioned by BBC Schools Programmes and first performed on sound radio during Spring Term 1966.

U.E. 14193.

17. *The Visions of Francesco Petrarca* Allegory for baritone, mime ensemble, chamber ensemble (flute, oboe, clarinet, horn, trumpet, trombone, two violins and cello) and school orchestra – (flute or recorder, oboe, clarinet, horn, trumpet, trombone, tuba, percussion [many players], strings.) Duration 65 minutes.

Text: Edmund Spenser's translation of seven sonnets by Petrarch (1304–74).

Six incidents of beautiful things destroyed by 'troublous fate' related by baritone with chamber ensemble; events gone through again in mime with school orchestra; all unite for final tableau.

Commissioned by 1966 York Festival. Composed between October 1965 and May 1966.

First performed in Church of St Michael-le-Belfrey, York, 15 June 1966, by Geoffrey Shaw, students of St John's College, York (mime), an amateur chamber ensemble, conducted by the composer, and the orchestra of Archbishop Holgate's Grammar School, York, conducted by Robin Black. The producer was David Henshaw, the designer Antony Denning.

U.E. 14176. Withdrawn for revision.

18. *Punch and Judy* a tragical comedy or comical tragedy in one act, for high soprano (Pretty Polly, later Witch), mezzo-soprano (Judy, later Fortune-Teller), high tenor (Lawyer), high baritone (Punch), low baritone (Choregos, later Jack Ketch), basso profundo (Doctor), and 5 mime dancers; on stage, a wind quintet (flute (doubling piccolo), oboe (doubling cor anglais and oboe d'amore), clarinet (doubling E♭ clarinet, bass clarinet and

soprano saxophone), horn and bassoon (doubling contra); in the pit, trumpet, trombone, harp, percussion (2 players), 2 violins, viola, cello and double bass. Duration 110 minutes.

Libretto by Stephen Pruslin.

Prologue, four scenes (each consisting of a melodrama and a quest for Pretty Poll) and epilogue.

Commissioned by English Opera Group. Composed between January 1966 and 8 January 1967. Dedicated to 'My pretty Poll'.

First performed by English Opera Group (Jenny Hill, Maureen Morelle, John Winfield, John Cameron, Geoffrey Chard and Wyndham Parfitt) conducted by David Atherton, Jubilee Hall, Aldeburgh, 8 June 1968. The producer was Anthony Besch, choreographer Alfred Rodrigues and designer Peter Rice.

Recorded (1980) by Phyllis Bryn-Julson, Jan de Gaetani, Philip Langridge, Stephen Roberts, David Wilson-Johnson, John Tomlinson and London Sinfonietta, conducted by David Atherton, on Etcetera KTC 2014.

U.E. 14191.

19. *Chorale from a Toy-Shop*

First version: for flute, oboe or clarinet, clarinet or cor anglais, horn or trombone, bassoon or tuba. Duration 2 minutes.

Commissioned by *Tempo* for Igor Stravinsky's 85th birthday and published in its 81st edition, summer 1967. Composed April 1967.

First performed by Lancaster University Chamber Group, All Saints Church, Lewes, 28 March 1979.

Second version: for 2 trumpets, horn, trombone and tuba. Duration 1–5 minutes.

First performed by Philip Jones Brass Ensemble, Queen Elizabeth Hall, 19 May 1978.

U.E. 16046.

20. *Monodrama* for soprano (Protagonist), speaker (Choregos), flute (doubling piccolo and alto flute), clarinet (doubling A♭, E♭

and bass clarinets), violin, cello and percussion (2 players). Duration 40 minutes.

Text by Stephen Pruslin.

Based on an early form of Greek tragedy in which a single actor takes on numerous dramatic functions.

Commissioned by Anglo-Austrian Music Society for the first concert of Pierrot Players. Completed April 1967. Dedicated to Peter Maxwell Davies.

First performed by Mary Thomas and Pierrot Players, conducted by the composer, Queen Elizabeth Hall, 30 May 1967.

Score withdrawn.

21. *Three Lessons in a Frame* for piano solo, 4 instruments (flute (doubling piccolo), clarinet, violin, cello) and percussion. Duration 20 minutes.

Explores visual image of a mould and its copy. The first two lessons, for piano alone and instruments alone respectively, are really the same work twice, except that whatever is implied but missing in one of them is to be found in its complement. In the third lesson the two interlock.

Commissioned by Macnaghten Concerts for 1967 Cheltenham Festival. Dedicated to Stephen Pruslin.

First performed by Stephen Pruslin and Pierrot Players, conducted by Peter Maxwell Davies. Town Hall, Cheltenham, 17 July 1967.

Score withdrawn.

22. *Nomos* for four amplified instruments (flute, clarinet, horn, bassoon) and orchestra – 4 flutes (2nd, 3rd and 4th doubling piccolo), 3 oboes (3rd doubling cor anglais), 3 clarinets (2nd and 3rd doubling E♭ clarinet, 3rd doubling bass clarinet), 3 bassoons (3rd doubling contra), 4 horns, 4 trumpets, 3 trombones, tuba, harp, celeste, percussion (6 players), 10 violas, 10 cellos, and 8 double basses. Duration 15 minutes.

Single movement in which the amplified instruments, as the

'lawgivers', lay down a continuous *cantus firmus* that orders both micro- and macrostructure.

Commissioned by BBC for 1968 Promenade Concerts. Composed winter 1967–8.

First performed by BBC Symphony Orchestra, conducted by Colin Davis, Royal Albert Hall, 23 August 1968.

Recorded (1994) by BBC Symphony Orchestra, conducted by Paul Daniel on Collins Classics 14142.

23. *Linoi*. Duration 10 minutes (all versions).

First version: for clarinet in A (with extension down to C) and piano.

Title implies 'a broken line'; single arch with piano playing pizzicato throughout.

Composed late summer 1968.

First performed by Alan Hacker and Stephen Pruslin at an ICA concert, Purcell Room, 11 October 1968.

Second version: the same with the addition of tape (Realization: Peter Zinovieff) and dancer.

First performed by Alan Hacker, Stephen Pruslin and Clover Roope, Queen Elizabeth Hall, 22 April 1969.

Third version: for clarinet and piano with cello.

First performed at 1981 Huddersfield Contemporary Music Festival by Alan Hacker, Peter Hill and Jennifer Ward-Clarke, Huddersfield Polytechnic Music Hall, 19 November 1981.

U.E. 15313.

24. *Four Interludes for a Tragedy* for basset clarinet in A and tape (Realization: Peter Zinovieff). Reworkings of the interludes in *Monodrama* (20); intended to frame the two halves of a concert. Duration about 4 minutes each.

Score prefaced with a quotation from Djuna Barnes's novel *Nightwood* (1936): 'With shocked protruding eyeballs, for which the tragic mouth seemed to pour forth tears.'

First performed by Alan Hacker, without tape, Conway Hall,

London, 18 October 1968; with tape, Queen Elizabeth Hall, 10 February 1969.
Recorded (1977) by Alan Hacker on L'Oiseau-Lyre DSLO 17. (LP deleted)
U.E. 16047.

25. *Verses for Ensembles* for woodwind quintet (piccolo doubling alto flute, oboe doubling cor anglais, clarinet doubling Eb clarinet, clarinet doubling bass clarinet, bassoon doubling contra), brass quintet (2 trumpets, horn, 2 trombones) and percussion (3 players). Duration 28 minutes.
Commissioned by London Sinfonietta. Composed winter 1968–9. Dedicated to Bill Colleran.
First performed by London Sinfonietta, conducted by David Atherton, Queen Elizabeth Hall, 12 February 1969.
Recorded by 1) London Sinfonietta, conducted by David Atherton (1974), on Decca HEAD 7 (LP deleted); 2) Netherlands Wind Ensemble, conducted by James Wood (1991), on Etcetera KTC 1130.
U.E. 15331.

26. *Some Petals from my Twickenham Herbarium* for piccolo, clarinet, viola, cello, piano and bells. Duration 2½ minutes.
Commissioned by Universal Edition to celebrate the 80th birthday of Dr Alfred A. Kalmus. Composed March 1969.
First performed by Pierrot Players, conducted by the composer, Queen Elizabeth Hall, 22 April 1969.
Recorded (1976 by a group of Spanish musicians, conducted by Cristobal Halffter on U.E. 15043 (ID 104).

27. *Down by the Greenwood Side* a dramatic pastoral for soprano (Mrs Green), actors (Father Christmas, St George, Bold Slasher, Dr Blood), mime (Jack Finney); flute (doubling piccolo and alto flute), clarinet (doubling Eb and bass clarinets), bassoon (doubling contra), cornet, trombone, euphonium, percussion

(one player), violin and cello. Duration 40 minutes.

Text by Michael Nyman based on the traditional English Mummers' Play and the ballad of the Cruel Mother.

One act divided into scenes devoted to Presenter, Combatants, Dispute, Lament, Cure and Quete, interspersed with various versions of the ballad.

Commissioned by Ian Hunter for the Brighton Festival Society. Composed winter 1968–9.

First performed in Festival Pavilion, West Pier, Brighton, 8 May 1969, by Jenny Hill and Music Theatre Ensemble, conducted by David Atherton. The producer was John Cox, the designer Antony Denning.

U.E. 15321.

28. *Cantata* for soprano, flute (doubling piccolo), clarinet (doubling high-pitched B♭ clarinet), violin (doubling viola), cello, piano (doubling celeste) and glockenspiel (doubling small bongo). Duration 11 minutes.

Text by the composer taken from tombstone inscriptions and translated from Sappho and *The Greek Anthology*.

Composed spring 1969. Dedicated to 'Jill and Robin' (Yapp).

First performed by Mary Thomas and Pierrot Players, conducted by the composer, Purcell Room, 12 June 1969.

U.E. 15344.

29. *Ut Heremita Solus*. An arrangement of the motet by Ockeghem (*c.* 1425–95); for flute (doubling piccolo and alto flute), clarinet (doubling bass clarinet), viola, cello, piano and glockenspiel. Duration 7 minutes.

First performed by Pierrot Players, conducted by the composer, Purcell Rooms, 12 June 1969.

U.E. 15366.

30. *Hoquetus David* An arrangement of the motet by Machaut (*c.* 1300); for flute (doubling piccolo), clarinet in C, violin, cello,

glockenspiel and bells. Duration 4 minutes.
First performed by Pierrot Players, conducted by the composer, Firth Hall, University of Sheffield, 22 October 1969.
U.E. 15368.

31. *Medusa*
First version: for flute (doubling piccolo), clarinet (doubling A♭ clarinet and soprano saxophone), viola, cello (all amplified), piano (doubling celeste), percussion, two electronic tapes (one synthesized sounds, the other an alto saxophone distorted) and shozyg (an instrument invented by Hugh Davies amplifying the sounds of small objects inside a container). Duration 21 minutes.
Commissioned by BBC for an Invitation Concert. Composed September 1969.
First performed by Pierrot Players with Peter Zinovieff (electronics), conducted by the composer, Firth Hall, University of Sheffield, 22 October 1969.
Score withdrawn.
Second version: the same except that viola doubles violin and shozyg is replaced by synthesizer. Duration 50 minutes.
Extended by parodies of Bach's Chorale Prelude on the Magnificat: *Meine Seele erhebt den Herren* and the Chorale *Wer nur den lieben Gott lässt walten*. Duration 10 minutes.
First performed by same artists, Queen Elizabeth Hall, 3 March 1970.

32. *Eight Lessons for Keyboards* Eight musical objects with instructions on how they might be realized. Durations variable.
First performed by Stephen Pruslin, doubling piano and celeste, Purcell Room, 13 January 1970, when he interspersed them between Beethoven's Bagatelles, Op. 119.
Not published.

33. *Signals* for clarinet and electronic sounds.
The player, on hearing a signal on tape, chooses from five

possible sets of responses. Duration of tape 45 minutes.
Commissioned by the Richard Demarco Gallery, Edinburgh.
First performed by Alan Hacker in the Demarco Gallery, August
1970.
Not published.

34. *Nenia: the Death of Orpheus* for soprano, three bass clarinets
(1st doubling B♭ clarinet), piano (doubling prepared piano) and
crotales. Duration 17 minutes.
Text by Peter Zinovieff.
Dramatic scene in five sections.
Commissioned by Jane Manning. Composed autumn 1970.
First performed by Jane Manning and Matrix (Alan Hacker, Ian
Mitchell, Francis Christou, Paul Crossley and Tristan Fry) at a
BBC Invitation Concert, Maida Vale Studios, London, 20
November 1970.
Recorded by 1) Jane Manning and Matrix (1973) on Decca
HEAD 7 (LP deleted); 2) Rosemary Hardy and Musikfabrik
NRW (1991) on Etcetera KTC 1130.
U.E. 15410.

35. *Dinah and Nick's Love Song* for three melody instruments and
harp. Duration 5 minutes.
Commissioned by Dinah and Nick Wood and dedicated to them.
Composed autumn 1970.
First public performance by Matrix at a BBC Invitation Concert,
Firth Hall, University of Sheffield, 26 October 1972.
U.E. 16040.

36. *Meridian* for mezzo-soprano, horn, cello, two 3-part choirs of
sopranos, 3 oboes (doubling cors anglais), 3 clarinets (doubling
bass clarinets), 2 harps, piano and percussion (2 players).
Duration 30 minutes.
Text: Christopher Logue's *The image of love* from *Wand and
Quadrant, Collection Merlin* (The Olympia Press, 1953), and lines

from Sir Thomas Wyatt's *Blame not, my lute* and *My lute awake*.
Commissioned by the London Sinfonietta. Composed Winter
1970–71.
First performed by Yvonne Minton, Barry Tuckwell, Jennifer
Ward-Clarke, members of London Sinfonietta Chorus and
London Sinfonietta, conducted by David Atherton, Queen
Elizabeth Hall, 26 February 1971.
Recorded (1991) by Mary King, Michael Thomson, Christopher
van Kampen, London Sinfonietta Voices and London
Sinfonietta, conducted by Oliver Knussen on NMC D0009.
U.E. 15430.

37. *Prologue* for tenor, bassoon, horn, 2 trumpets, tombone,
violin and double bass. Duration 8 minutes.
Text: the opening of the Watchman's speech from *Agamemnon* by
Aeschylus, translated by Philip Vellacott, Penguin, 1956.
Commissioned by 1971 English Bach Festival for Philip
Langridge and London Sinfonietta. Composed early 1971.
Dedicated 'to Michael and Aet' (Nyman) 'on the occasion of
Molly'.
First performed by Philip Langridge and London Sinfonietta
conducted by the composer, English Bach Festival, 18 April
1971.
U.E. 15491.

38. *An Imaginary Landscape* for 4 trumpets, 4 horns, 3 trom-
bones, tuba, 8 double-basses and percussion (4 players). Duration
17 minutes.
A single movement built from five different sound-blocks.
Commissioned by BBC for 1971 ISCM Festival in London.
Composed between January and May 1971. Dedicated 'to the
memory of my mother'.
First performed by BBC Symphony Orchestra, conducted by
Pierre Boulez, Royal Festival Hall, 2 June 1971.
Recorded (1994) by BBC Symphony Orchestra, conducted by

Paul Daniel on Collins Classics 14142.
U.E. 15474.

39. *The Fields of Sorrow* for 2 sopranos, chorus, 3 flutes, 3 cor anglais, 3 bass clarinets, 3 bassoons, horn, vibraphone and 2 pianos. Duration 9 minutes.
Text by Decimus Ausonius (*c.* 310–95) contained in Helen Waddell's *Mediaeval Latin Lyrics*, Constable, 1929.
Commissioned by Dartington Summer School of Music. Composed July 1971, revised February 1972.
First performed by students at Dartington Summer School, conducted by the composer, Dartington Hall, 7 August 1971.
Recorded (1974) by Jane Manning and London Sinfonietta, conducted by David Atherton on Decca HEAD 7. (LP deleted)
U.E. 15462.

40. *Tombeau in Memoriam Igor Stravinsky* for flute, clarinet, harp and string quartet. Duration 3 minutes.
Commissioned by *Tempo*. Composed September 1971.
First public performance by London Sinfonietta, conducted by Elgar Howarth, St John's, Smith Square, 17 June 1972.
U.E. 16045.

41. *Chronometer* for two asynchronous 4-track tapes. Realized by Peter Zinovieff. Duration 24 minutes.
Composed winter 1971–2.
First performed at a Redcliffe Concert, Queen Elizabeth Hall, 24 April 1972.
Recorded (1975) on Argo ZRG 790 (two-track). (LP deleted)

42. *Epilogue* for baritone, horn, 4 trombones and 6 tamtams (2 players). Duration 7 minutes.
Text: Shakespeare's *Full fathom five* (*The Tempest*).
Commissioned by Globe Playhouse Trust for Shakespeare's birthday. Completed 15 April 1972.

First performed by Michael Rippon and London Sinfonietta, conducted by the composer, Southwark Cathedral, 23 April 1972. U.E. 16056.

43. *The Triumph of Time* for orchestra – 3 flutes (3rd doubling piccolo), 3 oboes (2nd and 3rd doubling cor anglais), 3 clarinets (2nd and 3rd doubling bass clarinets), soprano saxophone (amplified), 2 bassoons (2nd doubling contra), 4 horns, 4 trumpets, 3 trombones, 2 tubas, piano, 2 harps, percussion (5 players), at least 20 violins, 9 violas, 9 cellos and 9 double basses. Duration 28 minutes.
Commissioned by the Royal Philharmonic Orchestra. Composed between summer 1971 and spring 1972.
First performed by Royal Philharmonic Orchestra, conducted by Lawrence Foster, Royal Festival Hall, 1 June 1972.
Recorded by 1) BBC Symphony Orchestra, conducted by Pierre Boulez (1975), on Argo ZRG 790 (LP deleted); 2) Philharmonia Orchestra, conducted by Elgar Howarth (1993), on Collins Classics 13872.
U.E. 15518.

44. *La Plage: Eight Arias of Remembrance* for soprano, 3 clarinets, piano and marimba. Duration 14 minutes.
Text taken from *La Plage* by Alain Robbe-Grillet.
Commissioned by BBC for an Invitation Concert. Composed summer 1972.
First performed by Jane Manning and Matrix, Firth Hall, University of Sheffield, 26 October 1972.
U.E. 15539.

45. *Grimethorpe Aria* for brass band (E♭ cornet, 8 B♭ cornets, flugel horn, 3 E♭ horns, 3 trombones, 2 euphoniums, 2 B♭ baritones, 2 EE♭ basses, 2 BB♭ basses. Duration 14 minutes.
Score prefaced with quotation from Blake's *Jerusalem* (Chapter 3, Plate 55, lines 57–8): 'Let the Indefinite be explored, and let

every Man be Judged by his own Works.'
Commissioned by Grimethorpe Colliery Band for 1973
Harrogate Festival. Composed between March and June 1973.
Dedicated to Elgar Howarth and the Grimethorpe Colliery Band.
First performed by Grimethorpe Colliery Band, conducted by
the composer, Royal Hall, Harrogate, 15 August 1973.
Recorded (1976) by Grimethorpe Colliery and Besses o' th' Barn
Bands, conducted by Elgar Howarth on Decca HEAD 14. (LP
deleted)
U.E. 15562.

46. *Chanson de Geste* for amplified sustaining instrument and
pre-recorded tape (Peter Zinovieff). Duration 10 minutes.
Related to *Grimethorpe Aria*. Contrasts 'a continuous element and
an intermittent, more percussive element'.
Commissioned by and dedicated to Fernando Grillo. Composed
May 1973.
First performed by Fernando Grillo (double bass), Perugia, July
1973.
U.E. 15561.
Score withdrawn.

47. *Five Chorale Preludes*. An arrangement of J.S. Bach's *Durch
Adam's Fall ist ganz verderbt, Wer nur den lieben Gott lässt walten,
Christus, der uns selig macht, Jesus, meine Zuversicht, Das alte Jahr
vergangen ist* for soprano, clarinet, basset horn and bass clarinet.
Duration 18 minutes.
First performed by Jane Manning and Matrix, Roundhouse,
London, 15 September 1975.
U.E. 15559.

48. *Melencolia 1* for solo clarinet in A, harp and 2 string orchestras (each containing 15 violins, 6 violas, 6 cellos and 4 double
basses). Duration *c*. 20 minutes.
Title refers to the engraving by Dürer, 1502.

Commissioned for Musica Nova 1976 by the Scottish National Orchestra Society. Completed July 1976. Dedicated to the memory of Tony Wright (of Universal Edition).

First performed by Alan Hacker and Scottish National Orchestra conducted by Alexander Gibson, Bute Hall, Glasgow University, 18 September 1976.

Recorded (1993) by Antony Pay and London Sinfonietta, conducted by Oliver Knussen on NMC D009.

U.E. 16128.

49. *For O, for O, the Hobby-horse is Forgot* a ceremony for six percussionists. Duration 27 minutes.

Title taken from Act III, scene 2 of *Hamlet*: 'Then there's hope a great man's memory may outlive his life half a year; but, by'r Lady, he must build churches, then, or else shall he suffer not thinking on, with the hobby-horse, whose epitaph is, "For O, for O, the hobby-horse is forgot." '

Commissioned by Les Percussions de Strasbourg. Dedicated to Andrew Rosner. Composed summer 1976.

First performed by Les Percussions de Strasbourg, Tokyo, 10 February 1978.

Recorded (1992) by Hague Percussion Ensemble on Etcetera KTC 1052.

U.E. 16137.

50. *Silbury Air* for flute (doubling piccolo and alto flute), oboe (doubling cor anglais), clarinet (doubling bass clarinet), bassoon (doubling contra), trumpet, horn, trombone, piano, harp, percussion (one player), 2 violins, viola, cello and double bass. Duration 18 minutes.

Score is prefaced by a Pulse Labyrinth.

Commissioned by The Koussevitzky Music Foundation in The Library of Congress for the Chamber Music Society of Lincoln Center to honour the centenary of the birth of Serge Koussevitzky. Completed 18 February 1977. Dedicated to the memory of Serge and Natalie Koussevitzsky.

First performed by London Sinfonietta, conducted by Elgar Howarth, Queen Elizabeth Hall, 9 March 1997.

Recorded (1987) by London Sinfonietta, conducted by Elgar Howarth, on Etcetera KTC 1052.

U.E. 16141.

51. *Pulse Field (Frames, Pulses and Interruptions)* Ballet in collaboration with Jaap Flier for 6 dancers and 9 musicians (3 bass trombones, 2 amplified double basses and percussion (4 players). Duration 35 minutes.

Title refers to way music and dance are built in small frames and sections, related to a flexible pulse and interrupted by relationships that develop between the performers.

Commissioned by Ballet Rambert.

First performed by Ballet Rambert at 1977 Aldeburgh Festival, Maltings, Snape, 25 June 1977. The designer was Nadine Baylis.

U.E. 16146.

52. *Bow Down* Music theatre for 5 actors and 4 musicians (bamboo flute, bamboo pipes, oboes, penny whistles and percussion). Duration 50 minutes.

Text by Tony Harrison based upon various versions of the ballad of the Two Sisters.

First performed by members of the National Theatre at Cottesloe Theatre, 5 July, 1977. The director was Walter Donohue, music director Dominic Muldowney, designer Jennifer Carey, choreographer Judith Paris.

U.E. 16180.

53. *Carmen Arcadiae Mechanicae Perpetuum* for flute (doubling piccolo), oboe, clarinet (doubling bass clarinet), bassoon (doubling contra), trumpet, horn, trombone, marimbaphone, piano or electric piano, 2 violins, viola, cello and double bass. Duration 12 minutes.

Six musical mechanisms juxtaposed many times without any form of transition.

Commissioned by London Sinfonietta. Composed autumn 1977. Dedicated 'To my friends the London Sinfonietta on the occasion of their tenth birthday'.

First performed by London Sinfonietta, conducted by the composer, Queen Elizabeth Hall, 24 January 1978.

Recorded (1987) by London Sinfonietta, conducted by Elgar Howarth, on Etcetera KTC 1052.

54. ... *agm* ... Music for 16 voices (4 S, 4 A, 4 T, 4 B) and 3 instrumental groups (high – 2 flutes (doubling piccolos), 2 oboes, clarinet, 2 trumpets, horn, 2 violins, viola; low – bass clarinet, bassoon, contra, 2 trombones, tuba, 2 cellos, double bass; punctuating – piano, 2 harps, percussion (3 players)). Duration 35 minutes.

Text: The Fayum fragments of Sappho with translations by Tony Harrison.

Commissioned by Ensemble InterContemporain. Composed between December 1978 and March 1979. Dedicated to Nicholas Snowman.

First performed by the John Alldis Choir and Ensemble InterContemporain, conducted by Pierre Boulez, Théâtre de la Ville, Paris, 9 April 1979.

Recorded 11–12 June 1982 at IRCAM, Centre Georges Pompidou, Paris, by the John Alldis Choir and the Ensemble InterContemporain, conducted by Pierre Boulez on Erato STU 71543. (LP deleted)

U.E. 16245.

55. *Choral Fragments from* ... *agm* ... for 16 voices. Duration 17 minutes.

An arrangement of the vocal parts of ... *agm* ...

First performed by John Alldis Choir, conducted by John Alldis, Concert Hall, Broadcasting House, London, 5 April 1979.

Not published separately.

56. *Mercure – Poses Plastiques* An arrangement of Satie's ballet for flute (doubling piccolo and alto flute), oboe (doubling cor anglais), clarinet (doubling bass clarinet), bassoon (doubling contra), trumpet, horn, trombone, piano, percussion (1 player), 2 violins, viola, cello and double bass. Duration 19 minutes.
Completed Raasay, 12 February 1980.
First performed by London Sinfonietta, conducted by Elgar Howarth. Queen Elizabeth hall, 4 April 1980.
U.E. 17606.

57. *On the Sheer Threshold of the Night* Madrigal for 4 solo voices (S, A (countertenor), T, B) and 12-part chorus. Duration 16 minutes.
Text: Boethius' *Stupet tergeminus novo* (*The Consolation of Philosophy*) contained in Helen Waddell's *Mediaeval Latin Lyrics*, Constable, 1929.
Score is headed by the inscription: 'In 524 Anicius Manlius Severinus Boethius, ex-consul and Roman senator, died by Order of Theodoric under torture in the dungeon of Pavia in his forty-fifth year.'
Commissioned by Hessischer Rundfunk, Frankfurt. Composed 1980.
First performed at Hessischer Rundfunk, May 1980, by John Alldis Choir, conducted by John Alldis, who also gave the British première at Bath Festival, St Andrew's Church, Mells (Somerset), 31 May 1981.
U.E. 16410.

58. *Clarinet Quintet* for clarinet, 2 violins, viola and cello. Duration 22 minutes.
Composed Raasay/Bagua di Lucca/Raasay, summer–autumn 1980. Dedicated to Sir William Glock.
First performed at 1981 Huddersfield Contemporary Music Festival by Alan Hacker and The Music Party, St Paul's Hall, Huddersfield, 21 November 1981.
U.E. 17324.

59. *Pulse Sampler* for oboe and claves.
Composed Summer 1981. Duration 8 minutes.
First performed at 1981 Huddersfield Contemporary Music
Festival by Melinda Maxwell and John Harrod, Huddersfield
Polytechnic Music Hall, 20 November 1981.
Recorded (1996) by Melinda Maxwell (oboe) and Richard
Benjafield (claves) on NMC DO415.
U.E. 16402.

60. *The Mask of Orpheus* A lyric tragedy in three acts; for 2 sopranos (The Oracle of the Dead (doubling Hecate) and First
Woman), 3 mezzo-sopranos (Euridice singer and puppet
(doubling Persephone) and Second Woman), contralto (Third
Woman), 3 tenors (Aristaeus singer and puppet (doubling
Charon) and First Priest), 2 high baritones (Orpheus singer and
puppet (doubling Hades)), baritone (Second Priest), bass-baritone (The Caller), basso profundo (Third Priest), mime troupe
and 12-part chorus (in pit). Orchestra: 3 flutes (1st doubling
piccolo, 2nd and 3rd piccolos and alto flutes), alto flute (doubling
bass flute), 3 oboes (1st doubling oboe d'amore, 2nd and 3rd cor
anglais), cor anglais (doubling bass oboe in C), 3 clarinets (1st
doubling E♭, 2nd E♭ and bass, 3rd bass clarinets), bass clarinet
(doubling contrabass clarinet), 3 soprano saxophones (doubling
bamboo pipes, recorders and conches), 3 bassoons (2nd and 3rd
doubling contra), contra bassoon, 4 trumpets, 4 horns, 6 trombones, 2 tubas, 3 harps (all amplified), small electric harp, 7-
string metal harp, *Noh* harp, electric mandolin, electric guitar
and bass guitar, organ, percussion (7 players), pre-recorded tapes.
Duration 3 hours 30 minutes.
Libretto by Peter Zinovieff.
Electronic material realized by Barry Anderson in association
with IRCAM.
Commissioned by English National Opera. Acts I and II
composed between autumn 1973 and spring 1975, Act III
between autumn 1981 and autumn 1983.

First performed by English National Opera, conducted by Elgar Howarth assisted by Paul Daniel, London Coliseum, 21 May 1986. The principal singers were Philip Langridge (Orpheus), Jean Rigby (Euridice), Tom McDonnell (Aristeus), Marie Angel (The Oracle of the Dead and Hecate) and Richard Angas (The Caller). The producer was David Freeman, the designer Jocelyn Herbert.

Recorded (1996) by Jon Garrison (Orpheus), Jean Rigby (Euridice), Alan Opie (Aristeus), Marie Angel (The Oracle of the Dead and Hecate) and Stephen Allen (The Caller), BBC Symphony Orchestra, conducted by Andrew Davis assisted by Martyn Brabbins, on NMC D050.

Full score U.E. 17680, vocal score U.E. 17682.

61. *Duets for Storab* for two flutes. Duration 6–7 minutes.
1. Urlar
2. Stark Pastoral.
3. Fanfare with Birds.
4. White Pastoral
5. From the Church of Lies.
6. Crumluath.

Composed Raasay, January 1983.

First performed by members of the Endymion Ensemble, Rosslyn Hill Chapel, London, 25 March 1984.

62. *Deowa* for soprano and clarinet. Duration 10 minutes.
Based on the phonemes contained in the title.
Composed early 1983.
First performed by Jane Manning and Alan Hacker, Wigmore Hall, 29 March 1983.
U.E. 17664.

63. *Yan Tan Tethera*, a 'mechanical pastorale' in one act for soprano (Hannah), bright tenor (Piper/Bad'un), light baritone (Allen), dark baritone (Caleb Raven), four children's voices (Jack

and Dick, Davie and Rab), a chorus of 13 sheep, flute (doubling alto flute), 2 oboes (2nd doubling cor anglais), 2 bassoons (2nd doubling contra), horn, harp, percussion (2 players), 3 violins, 2 violas, cellos and double bass. Duration 90 minutes.
Text by Tony Harrison.
Commissioned by the BBC for simultaneous transmission on BBC2 and Radio 3. Composed winter 1983–4.
First performed by Opera Factory/London Sinfonietta, conducted by Elgar Howarth, Queen Elizabeth Hall, 7 August 1986. The principal singers were Helen Charnock (Hannah), Omar Ebrahim (Alan), Richard Suart (Caleb) and Philip Doghan (Piper and Bad'un)). The director was David Freeman, the designer David Roper.
Full score U.E. 17684, vocal score U.E. 17686.

64. *Still Movement* for 13 solo strings – 8 violins, 2 violas, 2 cellos and double bass. Duration *c*. 10 minutes.
Commissioned by the 1984 City of London Festival for the Polish Chamber Orchestra. Composed March and April 1984.
First performed by Polish Chamber Orchestra, conducted by Jerzy Maksymiuk, Guildhall Old Library, 20 July 1984.
U.E. 17676.

65. *Secret Theatre* for 14 players. Dramatis personae: flute (doubling piccolo) oboe, clarinet, bassoon (doubling contra), trumpet in C (doubling piccolo trumpet in B♭), horn, trombone, percussion (1 player), piano, 2 violins, viola, cello and double bass. Duration 28 minutes.
Commissioned by the London Sinfonietta. Composed between 3 May and 17 September, 1984. Dedicated to Sheila (Birtwistle).
First performed by London Sinfonietta, conducted by David Atherton, Queen Elizabeth Hall, 18 October 1984.
Recorded by 1) London Sinfonietta, conducted by Elgar Howarth (1987), on Etcetera KTC 1052; 2) Ensemble InterContemporain, conducted by Pierre Boulez (1993), on

Deutsche Grammophon 439 910–2; 3) Musikfrabrik NRW, conducted by Johannes Kalitzke (1995), on Koch International CP 999 360-2-2.
U.E. 17917.

66. *Songs by Myself* for soprano, flute (doubling alto flute), piano, vibraphone, violin, viola, cello and double bass. Duration *c*. 10 minutes.
Text by the composer.
Composed September 1984. 'Affectionately dedicated to my godson Thomas Michael Raphael Mustill in the year of his christening, 1984.
First performed by Penelope Walmsley-Clark and London Sinfonietta, conducted by the composer, Queen Elizabeth Hall, 18 October 1984.
U.E. 17918.

67. *Berceuse de Jeanne* for piano. Lasts as long as it takes for the baby to fall asleep.
Composed March 1985.
U.E. 17954. (Contained in album *Studio 21, Vol.1*).

68. *Words Overheard* for soprano, flute, oboe, bassoon, 12 violins, 4 violas, 4 cellos and 2 double basses. Duration *c*. 8 minutes.
Text by the composer.
Commissioned by the Scottish Chamber Orchestra. Composed autumn 1985. Dedicated to Brigitte Schiffer.
First performed by Penelope Walmsley-Clark and Scottish Chamber Orchestra, conducted by the composer, City Hall, Glasgow, 17 November 1985.
U.E. 17982.

69. *Earth Dances* for orchestra – 3 flutes (2nd and 3rd doubling piccolo, 3rd doubling alto flute), 3 oboes (3rd doubling cor anglais), 3 clarinets, (2nd and 3rd doubling E♭ clarinet, 3rd

doubling bass clarinet), 3 bassoons (2nd and 3rd doubling contra), 4 horns, 2 trumpets, 4 trombones, 2 tubas, piano, 2 harps, percussion (5 players), 30 violins, 9 violas, 9 cellos and 9 double basses. Duration 38 minutes.
Commissioned by the BBC. Composed during 1985 and completed 9 February 1986.
First performed by BBC Symphony Orchestra, conducted by Peter Eötvös, Royal Festival Hall, 14 March 1986.
Recorded by 1) BBC Symphony Orchestra, conducted by Peter Eötvös (1991), on Collins Classics 20012; 2) Cleveland Orchestra, conducted by Christoph von Dohnányi (1996), on Argo 452 104-2
U.E. 18464.

70. *Hector's Dawn* for piano. Duration *c*. 2 minutes.
'Chordal outer sections frame a twining double melody'.
Composed 19 February 1987. 'Written for Hector Snowman by his godfather Harrison Birtwistle on the occasion of his first birthday.'
U.E. 18776.

71. *Endless Parade* for trumpet, vibraphone and strings – 14 violins, 4 violas, 4 cellos and 2 double basses. Duration 20 minutes.
Commissioned by Paul Sacher. Completed 15 March 1987.
First performed by Håkan Hardenberger (trumpet) and the Collegium Musicum, conducted by Paul Sacher, Zürich, 1 May 1987.
Recorded (1990) by Håkan Hardenberger, Paul Patrick and BBC Philharmonic Orchestra, conducted by Elgar Howarth on Philips 432 075-2.
U.E. 18520.

72. *Fanfare for Will* for 3 trumpets, 4 horns, 3 trombones and tuba. Duration 2½ minutes.
Commissioned by the Shakespeare Globe Trust. Composed June

1987. 'Written for Sam Wanamaker'.
First performed by BBC Philharmonic Orchestra, conducted by the composer, Royal Festival Hall, 10 July 1987.
U.E. 18761.

73. *Les Hoquets du Gardien de la Lune*, an arrangement of Machaut's *Hoquetus David* for orchestra – 2 flutes, 2 oboes, 2 clarinets, 4 horns, 3 trumpets, 3 trombones, tuba, percussion (2 players), 18 violins, 6 violas, 6 cellos and 4 double basses. Duration *c.* 8 minutes.
Commissioned by the South Bank Centre. Composed summer 1987.
First performed by English Northern Philharmonia, conducted by Elgar Howarth, Queen Elizabeth Hall, 6 September 1987.
Unpublished.

74. *Four Songs of Autumn* for soprano and string quartet. Duration 6 minutes. Texts taken from *The Penguin Book of Japanese Verse*, translated by Geoffrey Bownas and Anthony Thwaite.
Composed between December 1987 and January 1988 for the 20th anniversary of the London Sinfonietta.
First performed by Sarah Leonard and members of London Sinfonietta, Royal Festival Hall, 24 January 1988.
U.E. 18794.

75. *An die Musik* for soprano, flute (doubling piccolo), oboe, clarinet, bassoon, percussion (1 player), 2 violins, viola, cello and double bass. Duration *c.* 5 minutes.
Text by Rainer Maria Rilke.
Commissioned by the South Bank Centre to mark the 80th birthday of Sir William Glock. Composed April 1988.
First performed by Elizabeth Laurence and London Sinfonietta, conducted by the composer, Queen Elizabeth Hall, 4 May 1988.
U.E. 18831.

76. *Machaut à ma Manière*, an arrangement of *O Livoris Feritas, Hoquetus David* and an Amen from *La Messe de Nostre Dame* by Machaut for orchestra – 2 flutes (both doubling piccolo), 2 oboes (2nd doubling cor anglais), 2 clarinets (2nd doubling E♭ clarinet), 2 bassoons (2nd double contra), 4 horns, 3 trumpets (1st doubling piccolo trumpet), 2 trombones, tuba, percussion (2 players), not fewer than 18 violins, 6 violas, 6 cellos and 4 double basses. Duration *c.* 10 minutes.
Commissioned by the Hamburg Philharmonic Orchestra (Philharmonisches Staatsorchester Hamburg). Composed August 1988.
First performed by Hamburg Philharmonic Orchestra, conducted by Gerd Albrecht in the Musikhalle, Hamburg, 10 March 1990.
U.E. 19152.

77. *Salford Toccata* for brass band – soprano cornet in E♭, 8 cornets in B♭, flugel horn in B♭, 3 horns in E♭, 2 baritones, 2 trombones, bass trombone, 2 euphoniums, 2 E♭ basses, 2BB♭ basses. Duration *c.* 15 minutes.
Commissioned by Keith Wilson, Head of the Department of Performing Arts and Media Studies, Salford College of Technology, for College Brass Band, conductor Roy Newsome. Completed 15 February 1989.
First performed by Salford College Brass Band, conducted by Elgar Howarth, Salford College of Technology, 12 April 1989.
U.E. 19183.

78. *White and Light* for soprano, 2 clarinets, viola, cello and double bass. Duration 5 minutes.
Text by Paul Celan, translated by Michael Hamburger.
Commissioned by the Composers Ensemble. Composed March 1989.
First performed by Mary Wiegold and Composers Ensemble, conducted by John Woolrich, Brighton Festival, 13 May 1989.

Recorded (1992) by Mary Wiegold and Composers Ensemble, conducted by Dominic Muldowney, on NMC D003.
U.E. 19223.

79. *The Wine Merchant Robin of Mere* for male voice and piano. Duration *c*. 3 minutes.
Text by the composer.
One of several drinking songs commissioned by Yapp Brothers to celebrate their 20th anniversary as importers of wine from the Rhône and Loire. (Others are by Peter Maxwell Davies, Colin Matthews, Dominic Muldowney and John Woolrich.) Composed January 1989.
First performed by Geoffrey Dolton (baritone) and John Leneham (piano) in *Tasting Notes* on BBC Radio 3, Boxing Day, 1989.
Published by Yapp Brothers of Mere, Wiltshire in *Yapp '89*.

80. *Ritual Fragment* for flute, oboe, clarinet, bassoon, horn, trumpet, bass trumpet, piano, bass drum, 2 violins, viola, cello and double bass. Duration 11 minutes.
Commissioned by London Sinfonietta for the Michael Vyner memorial concert. Composed April 1990. Dedicated to the memory of Michael Vyner.
First performed by London Sinfonietta, Royal Opera House, Covent Garden, 6 May 1990.
Recorded by 1) London Sinfonietta (1993) on NMC D009; 2) Musikfabrik NRW (1995) on Koch International CPO 999 360-2-2.
U.E. 19413.

81. *Gawain*, opera in two acts for 2 sopranos (Morgan le Fay and Guinevere), mezzo-soprano (Lady de Hautdesert), countertenor (Bishop Baldwin), 2 tenors (Arthur and Ywain), 2 baritones (Gawain and The Fool), bass-baritone (Green Knight/Bertilak), bass (Agravain), chorus, 3 flutes (3rd doubling piccolo), 3 oboes,

(3rd doubling cor anglais), 3 clarinets (2nd doubling E♭ clarinet, 3rd double contrabass clarinet), 3 bassoons (all doubling swanee whistles, 3rd doubling contra), 4 horns, 3 trumpets (1st and 2nd doubling piccolo trumpet, 3rd doubling flugel horn), 3 trombones, 3 tubas (1st doubling euphonium), timpani, percussion (4 players), cimbalom, harp, 24 violins, 9 violas, 9 cellos and 9 double basses. Duration of original version *c*. 180 minutes; duration of revised version *c*. 140 minutes.

Text by David Harsent based on the medieval romance, *Sir Gawain and the Green Knight*.

Commissioned by the Royal Opera House, Covent Garden. Composed between 1 April 1989 and 15 January 1991. Dedicated to Peter Heyworth.

First performed by The Royal Opera, conducted by Elgar Howarth, Royal Opera House, 30 May 1991. The singers were Marie Angel (Morgan), Penelope Walmsley-Clark (Guinevere), Elizabeth Laurence (Lady de Hautdesert), Kevin Smith (Baldwin), Richard Greager (Arthur), Lynton Atkinson (Ywain), François Le Roux (Gawain), Omar Ebrahim (The Fool), John Tomlinson (Bertilak), Clive Bayley (Agravain) and The Sixteen, directed by Harry Christophers. The director was Di Trevis, the designer Alison Chitty.

Revised version recorded (1994) by Marie Angel, Penelope Walmsley-Clark, Anne Howells, Kevin Smith, Richard Greager, John Marsden, François Le Roux, Omar Ebrahim, John Tomlinson, Alan Ewing, the Chorus and Orchestra of the Royal Opera House, conducted by Elgar Howarth, on Collins Classics 70412.

Full score U.E. 19701, vocal score U.E. 19703.

82. *Four Poems by Jaan Kaplinski* for soprano, flute, oboe, clarinet, bassoon, horn, trumpet, piano, harp, 2 violins, viola, cello and double bass. Duration *c*. 9 minutes.

Text by Jaan Kaplinski translated from the Estonian by Sam Hamill and the author.

Commissioned by the Aldeburgh Festival. Composed March 1991. 'Dedicated with affection to my grandson Cecil'.
First performed by Sarah Leonard and London Sinfonietta, conducted by the composer, Maltings, Snape, 19 June 1991.
U.E. 19717.

83. *Gawain's Journey* for orchestra – scoring as for the opera, except that no swanee whistles are required. Duration *c.* 25 minutes.
First performed by English Northern Philharmonia, conducted by Elgar Howarth, Vienna, 21 October 1991.
Recorded (1993) by Philharmonia Orchestra, conducted by Elgar Howarth, on Collins Classics 13872.
U.E. 19720.

84. *Movement for String Quartet (Frieze I)* Duration *c.*3 minutes.
Written for Alfred Schlee's 90th birthday. Composed September 1991.
First performed by Arditti Quartet, Vienna, 18 November 1991.
Not published separately.

85. *An Interrupted Endless Melody* for oboe and piano. Duration *c.* 5 minutes.
Composed October 1991. Dedicated to the memory of Janet Craxton.
First performed by Nicholas Daniel (oboe) and Julius Drake (piano), BBC Concert Hall, Broadcasting House, 7 November 1991.
B.&H.: ISMN M-060-10660-6 (playing score).

86. *Antiphonies* for piano and orchestra – 3 flutes (2nd and 3rd doubling piccolo), 3 oboes (3rd doubling cor anglais), 3 clarinets (2nd doubling E♭ clarinet, 3rd double bass clarinet), 3 bassoons (3rd doubling contra), 4 horns, 4 trumpets, 2 trombones, tuba, contrabass tuba, 2 harps, percussion (4 players), 24 violins, 8 violas, 8 cellos and 8 double basses. Duration 34 minutes.

Commissioned by Vincent Meyer for the Philharmonia
Orchestra and Betty Freeman for the Los Angeles Philharmonic
Orchestra. Completed 7 July 1992. Dedicated to the memory of
Howard Hartog.
First performed by Joanna MacGregor and the Philharmonia
Orchestra, conducted by Pierre Boulez, Paris, 5 May 1993.
Recorded (1994) by Joanna MacGregor and Dutch Radio
Philharmonic Orchestra, conducted by Michael Gielen, on
Collins Classics 14142.
U.E. 19780.

87. *Five Distances for Five Instruments* (flute, oboe, clarinet, horn
and bassoon). Duration 14 minutes.
Commissioned by the South Bank Centre. Composed July and
August 1992. Dedicated to David Sylvester.
First performed by Ensemble InterContemporain, Purcell Room,
7 May 1993.
Recorded (1993) by Ensemble InterContemporain on Deutsche
Grammophon 439 910-2.
U.E. 19738.

88. *Three Settings of Celan* (*White and Light, Night, Tenebrae*) for
soprano, 2 clarinets, viola, cello and double bass. Duration *c.* 14
minutes.
Texts by Paul Celan, translated by Michael Hamburger.
Composed August 1992.
First performed by Mary Wiegold and Composers Ensemble,
conducted by the composer, Purcell Room, 18 September 1992.
Recorded (1993) by Christine Whittlesey and Ensemble
InterContemporain, conducted by Pierre Boulez, on Deutsche
Grammophon 439 910-2.
U.E. 16558.

89. *Three Movements for String Quartet* (*Frieze II and 2 Fantasias*)
Duration *c.* 10 minutes.

Commissioned by Antwerp 1993, Cultural Capital of Europe, for the Arditti Quartet.
Composed September 1993.
First performed by Arditti Quartet, Antwerp, 8 November 1993.
U.E. 19749.

90. *The Second Mrs Kong*, opera in two acts for high soprano (4th Model), 2 lyric sopranos (Mirror and Euridice), 2 sopranos (Pearl and 3rd Model), 2 mezzo-sopranos (Inanna and 2nd Model)), low mezzo-soprano (1st Model), contralto (Madame Lena), countertenor (Orpheus), light tenor (Swami Zumzum), tenor (Kong), 2 baritones (Vermeer and Mr Dollarama), bass baritone (Anubis), bass (Monstrous Messenger), chorus, 2 flutes (1st doubling alto flute, 2nd doubling piccolo), 2 oboes (2nd doubling cor anglais), 2 clarinets (2nd doubling E♭ clarinet), alto and tenor saxophones, 2 bassoons (2nd doubling contra), 4 horns, 2 trumpets, 2 tubas (1st doubling euphonium), cimbalom, accordion, vibraphone, marimba, percussion (2 players), 16 violins, 6 violas, 6 cellos and 6 double basses.
Text by Russell Hoban.
Commissioned by Glyndebourne Touring Opera. Composed 1993/4.
First performed by Glyndebourne Touring Opera, conducted by Elgar Howarth, Glyndebourne, 24 October 1994. The principal singers were Philip Langridge (Kong), Helen Field (Pearl), Michael Chase (Orpheus), Stephen Page (Anubis and Death of Kong), Omar Ebrahim (Vermeer), Phyllis Cannan (Innana), Robert Poulton (Mr Dollarama), Kevin West (Swami Zumzum), Deborah York (Mirror), Nuala Willis (Madame Lena) and Liza Pulman (Euridice). The director and designer was Tom Cairns.
Full score U.E. 16549, vocal score U.E. 16548.

91. *Fanfare for Glyndebourne* for 4 trumpets, 4 horns, 2 trombones, contrabass trombone, tuba and 4 timpani (1 player).
Composed April 1994.

First performed by members of London Philharmonic Orchestra, conducted by Andrew Davies, Glyndebourne, 28 May 1994.
Unpublished.

92. *With Letter and Clock* for soprano, 2 clarinets, viola, cello and double bass. Duration 4 minutes.
Text by Paul Celan, translated by Michael Hamburger.
Written for Birtwistle's inauguration as Henry Purcell Professor of Composition at King's College, London.
First performed by Mary Wiegold and Composers Ensemble, conducted by the composer, King's College, 21 November 1994.
Not published separately.

93. *The Cry of Anubis* for tuba and orchestra – 2 flutes (both doubling piccolo), 2 oboes (2nd doubling cor anglais), 2 clarinets, 2 bassoons, 4 horns, 2 trumpets, percussion (2 players) harp and strings. Duration 13 minutes.
Commissioned by London Philharmonic Orchestra. Composed November and December 1994.
First performed by Owen Slade and London Philharmonic Orchestra, conducted by Elgar Howarth, Queen Elizabeth Hall, 16 January 1995.
B.&H.: ISMN M-060-10340-7 (study score)

94. *Hoquetus Petrus* for 2 flutes (1st doubling piccolo) and piccolo trumpet. Duration *c*. 2 minutes.
Written for the 70th birthday of Pierre Boulez. Composed February 1995.
First performed by members of the Chicago Symphony Orchestra, Symphony Centre, Chicago, 30 March 1995.
B.&H.: ISMN M-060-10794-8 (score and parts)

95. *Panic* for alto saxophone, drummer and orchestra of wind and percussion – 3 flutes (2nd and 3rd doubling piccolo), 3

oboes (3rd doubling cor anglais), 2 clarinets, bass clarinet, 3 bassoons (3rd doubling contra), 4 trumpets, 4 horns, 3 trombones, tuba, timpani and percussion (1 player). Duration *c*. 18 minutes.
Commissioned by the BBC for the centenary season of the Henry Wood Promenade Concerts. Completed 18 July 1995.
First performed by John Harle, Paul Clarvis and BBC Symphony Orchestra, conducted by Andrew Davis, Royal Albert Hall, 16 September 1995.
Recorded by same artists (October 1995) on Philips 452 104-2.
B.&H.: ISMN M-060-10617-0 (study score).

96. *Todtnauberg* for soprano, 2 clarinets, viola, cello and double bass. Duration 6 minutes.
Text by Paul Celan, translated by Michael Hamburger.
Commissioned by the BBC for the Fairest Isle Songbook. Composed November 1995.
First performed by Susan Roberts and an ensemble conducted by the composer, BBC Radio 3, 10 December 1995.
Not published separately.

97. *Slow Frieze* for solo piano, piccolo, oboe, clarinet, bassoon, trumpet, horn trombone, 2 violins, viola, cello, double bass and percussion (1 player). Duration *c*. 10 minutes.
Commissioned by the South Bank Centre on behalf of the London Sinfonietta.
Composed December 1995. 'For Rory 25 Dec. 95.'
First performed by Joanna MacGregor and London Sinfonietta, conducted by Markus Stenz, Queen Elizabeth Hall, 26 April 1996.
B.&H.

98. *An Eye, open* for soprano, 2 clarinets, viola, cello and double bass. Duration 2½ minutes.
Text by Paul Celan, translated by Michael Hamburger.
Written for Paul Sacher's 90th birthday. Composed January 1996.

First performed by Christine Whittlesey and Ensemble InterContemporain, conducted by Pierre Boulez, Basel, 27 April 1996.
Not published separately.

99. *Nine Setting of Celan* (*Thread Suns, White and Light, Psalm, With Letter and Clock, An Eye, open, Todtnauberg, Tenebrae, Night, Give the Word*) for soprano, 2 clarinets, viola, cello and double bass. Duration *c*. 35 minutes.
Texts by Paul Celan, translated by Michael Hamburger.
Thread Suns and *Psalm* commissioned by the City of Witten for the Wittener Tage für neue Kammermusik 1996. Composed between March 1989 and January 1996.
First performed (in German) by Claudia Barainsky and Klangforum Wien, conducted bu Johannes Kalitzke as part of *Pulse Shadows*, Witten, 28 April 1996.
B.&H.: ISMN M-060-10619-4 (full score).

100. *Nine Movements for String Quartet* (4 *Friezes* and 5 *Fantasias*)
Duration *c*. 32 minutes.
Movements 4, 5, 6, 7 and 8 (*Friezes 2* and *4, Fantasias 1, 3* and *5*) commissioned for the Arditti Quartet by the South Bank Centre, London, Vienna Konzerthaus, WDR for the Wittener Tage für Neue Kammermusik and the Holland Festival. Composed between September 1991 and January 1996.
First performed by Arditti Quartet as part of *Pulse Shadows*, Witten, 28 April 1996.
B.&H.

101. *Pulse Shadows*, meditations on Paul Celan for soprano, string quartet and ensemble (2 clarinets, viola, cello and double bass). Duration *c*. 67 minutes.
Alternates *Nine Movements for String Quartet* and *Nine Settings of Celan*.
First performed by Claudia Barainsky, Arditti Quartet and

Klangforum Wien, conducted by Johannes Kalitzke, Witten, 28 April 1996.
B.&H.: ISMN M-060-10616-3 (study score)

102. *Bach Measures*, arrangement of Chorale Preludes from Bach's *Orgel-Büchlein* for flute (doubling alto flute and piccolo), oboe (doubling cor anglais), clarinet (doubling bass clarinet), bassoon (doubling contra), horn, trumpet, trombone, bass trombone, vibraphone, glockenspiel, 2 violins, viola, cello and double bass. Duration 23 minutes.
1. *Nun komm' der Heiden Heiland'* 2. *Ich ruf zu dir, Herr Jesu Christ* 3. *Herr Gott, nun schleuss Himmel auf* 4. *Christe, du Lamm Gottes* 5. *Erstanden ist der heil'ge Christe* 6. *In dir ist Freude* 7. *Oh Mensch, bewein dein' Sunde gross* 8. *Durch Adam's Fall is ganze verderbt.*
Commissioned by the London Sinfonietta. Composed March 1996.
First performed by Richard Alston Dance Company and London Sinfonietta, conducted by Diego Masson, Queen Elizabeth Hall, 4 May 1996. (In this performance the order of the movements was 1-5-6-4-2-3-7-8).
B.&H.

103. *Exody 23: 59: 59* for orchestra – 3 flutes (2nd and 3rd doubling piccolo and pitchpipe, 3rd doubling alto flute), 3 oboes (3rd doubling cor anglais), 3 clarinets (1st doubling E♭ clarinet, 2nd doubling bass clarinet, 3rd doubling contrabass clarinet), 3 bassoons (3rd doubling contra), soprano saxophone, alto saxophone, 4 horns, 4 trumpets, 3 trombones, 2 tubas, percussion (5 players), 2 harps, electric piano, 30 violins, 12 violas, 10 cellos and 8 double basses. Duration *c.* 35 minutes.
Commissioned by the Chicago Symphony Orchestra. Composed between autumn 1996 and late summer 1997.
First performed by Chicago Symphony Orchestra, conducted by Daniel Barenboim, Symphony Centre, Chicago, 5 February 1998.
B.&H.: ISMN M-060-10795-5 (study score)

104. *Harrison's Clocks*, four pieces for piano. Duration *c.* 12 minutes.
Composed between November 1997 and March 1998.
First performed by Joanna MacGregor at the ISCM World Music Days in Manchester, Bridgewater Hall, 19 April 1998.
B.&H.

Other Music (none published)
Sad Song (1971), a modal piano piece for his eldest son Adam.
The Offence (1973), music for Sidney Lumet's film.
Untitled Piece (1979), for Bill Colleran's 50th birthday.
National Theatre Logo (1980), for 11 wind instruments and timpani.
Amadeus, As You Like It, The Cherry Orchard (with Dominic Muldowney), *The Country Wife, The Double Dealer, Hamlet, Herod* (with Dominic Muldowney), *The Oresteia, Tamburlaine the Great, The Trojan War Will Not Take Place, Volpone*: music for productions at the National Theatre (1976–83).

Bibliography

A selection of articles, reviews and studies published since 1983

Adlington, Robert, 'Antiphonies' (review of full score), *Music Review*, 53/i (February 1992), pp. 71–3

—— 'The Triumph of Time, Gawain's Journey' (review of compact disc), *Musical Times* (October 1993), p. 595

—— 'Gawain' (review of revival), *Musical Times* (July 1994), p. 463

—— 'Antiphonies, Nomos, An Imaginary Landscape' (review of compact disc), *Musical Times* (June 1995), p. 312

—— 'Grammar-school boys' (review of compact discs of music by Maxwell Davies and Birtwistle), *Musical Times* (January 1996), pp. 35–7

—— 'Harrison Birtwistle's recent music', *Tempo* (April 1996), pp. 2–8

—— 'Summary justice' (review of 'Secret Theatres'), *Musical Times* (July 1996), pp. 31–4

Bruce, David, 'Challenging the system' (study of *Panic*), *Musical Times* (April 1996), pp. 11–16

Bye, Anthony, 'Birtwistle's *Gawain*', *Musical Times* (May 1991)

Clements, Andrew, 'Harrison Birtwistle – a progress report at 50', *Musical Times* (March 1884), pp. 136–9

—— 'Birtwistle counts sheep' (a review of *Yan Tan Tethera*), *Musical Times* (August 1986)

Cross, Jonathan, 'Issues of Analysis in Birtwistle's *Four Songs of Autumn*', in M. Finnessy and R. Wright, eds., *New Music '89* (Oxford University Press, 1989), pp. 16–23.

—— 'In Defence of *Punch*', *Opera*, Vol. 44, No. 6 (June 1993), pp. 644–5

—— 'The Challenge of Modern Music: Birtwistle's *Refrains and Choruses*', in A. Pople. ed. *Theory, Analysis and Meaning in Music* (Cambridge University Press, 1994), pp. 184–94

—— 'The Action Never Stops, It Only Changes' (*The Second Mrs Kong*), *Musical Times* (November 1994), pp. 698–703

—— 'Lines and Circles: On Birtwistle's *Punch and Judy* and *Secret Theatre*', *Musical Analysis*, Vol. 13, Nos 2–3 (July/October 1994), pp. 203–25

—— '*Ritual Fragment* di Harrison Birtwistle', in Paulo Cecchi, ed., *Catalogo Biennale Musica 1995* (Venice 1995)

—— 'From Opera House to Concert Hall' (review of *The Cry of Anubis*), *Tempo* (April 1995), p. 37

—— 'Thoughts on First Hearing Sir Harrison Birtwistle's *Panic*', *Tempo* (January 1996), pp. 34–5

—— 'A Truly Perfect Knight' (review of compact disc of *Gawain*), *Musical Times* (September 1996), p. 33

—— 'Birtwistle's Secret Theatres' in C. Ayrey and M. Everist, eds., *Analytical Strategies and Musical Interpretation* (Cambridge University Press, 1997)

Ford, Andrew, 'The reticence of intuition – Sir Harrison Birtwistle', in *Composer to Composer: Conversations about Contemporary Music* (London, Quartet Books, 1993), pp. 52–9

Gavin, Thomas, 'Brave New Worlds', *Musical Times* (June 1994)

Griffiths, Paul, 'Harrison Birtwistle', in *New Sounds, New Personalities: British Composers of the 1980s* (London, Faber and Faber, 1985), pp. 186–94

Hall, Michael, *Birtwistle* (London, Robson Books, 1984)

—— 'The Sanctity of the Context – Hall on Recent Birtwistle', *Musical Times* (January 1988), pp. 14–16

—— '*Pulse Shadows*', *Tempo* (March 1998)

Hewett, Ivan, 'The Second Coming', *Musical Times* (January 1995), pp. 46–7

Marks, Anthony, '*The Mask of Orpheus*' (review of première),

Musical Times (July 1986), p. 397

—— *Yan Tan Tethera* (review of première), *Musical Times* (September 1986), p. 570

Pettit, Stephen, 'Birtwistle's Secret Theatres', *Opera* (April 1996), pp. 366–9

Samuel, Rhian, 'Birtwistle's *Gawain*; An essay and a diary', *Cambridge Opera Journal*, vol. 4, no. 2 (1992), pp. 163–78

Smalley, Roger, *'The Mask of Orpheus'*, *Tempo* (summer 1986), p. 41

Taylor, Michael, 'Birtwistle's first *The Triumph of Time*', *Mitteilung der Paul Sacher Stiftung*, No. 8 (March 1995), pp. 17–21

Warnaby, John, *'Secret Theatre'* (review), *Tempo* (March 1985), pp. 25–7

—— 'The theatre of nature – *Earth Dances*', *Tempo* 157 (1986), pp. 43–4

—— *'Endless Parade'* (review), *Tempo* (June 1988)

—— 'Having his way with Machaut – Harrison Birtwistle's *Machaut à ma manière*', *Tempo* 173 (1990), pp. 68–70

Whittall, Arnold, 'The Geometry of Comedy' (essay on *Secret Theatre*), *Musical Times* (January 1993) pp. 17–19

—— 'Comparatively Complex: Birtwistle, Maxwell Davies and Modernist Analysis', *Music Analysis*, vol. 13, no. 1 (1994) pp. 139–59

—— 'Modernist Aesthetics, Modernist Music – Some Analytical Perspectives', in *Music Theory in Concept and Practice* (University of Rochester Press, 1997), pp. 157–80

Wright, David, 'Clicks, Clocks and Claques: Birtwistle at 60', *Musical Times* (July 1994) pp. 427–31

Index of Works

Numbers in brackets refer to the order in which works appear in the Catalogue of Works pp.154–91.

General Index